D1378661

On Our Side

On Our Side

Order, authority and
interaction in school

Edited by
GERALD HAIGH

Maurice Temple Smith

First published in Great Britain in 1979
by Maurice Temple Smith Ltd
37 Great Russell Street, London WC1

ISBN 0 85117 176 1 cased/177 X paperback

Typeset by Input Typesetting Ltd
Printed in Great Britain by
Billing & Sons Ltd
London, Guildford & Worcester

Contents

Introduction

GERALD HAIGH

More than one writer in this symposium has ventured, in an attempt at definition, into the classical roots of the word 'discipline', and almost all have acknowledged that the label denotes a concept with hazy boundaries. Many people, I suppose, will be scornful of this sort of sophistry. Discipline is about keeping order, is it not? And surely the teacher must be able to keep order before he can teach? When my grandfather heard, twenty years ago, that I was going to teacher training college, he supposed that they would tell me how to keep order, and implicit in what he said was the feeling that everything else followed from that.

Mind you, it seems to me that teachers often make every appearance of subscribing to the same view. *Control* the class, then *teach* the class is a common theme passed on from one teaching generation to another, with the accompanying notion that the teacher who cannot control never gets to the point of being able to teach. Often, too, there is implicit in this scenario the assumption that control is established and maintained by force − albeit, ideally, force of personality rather than the physical kind. This leads to the belief that the admirable teacher − or indeed the admirable youth worker or sports coach − is the one whose own will is strong enough to subjugate others. And going on one step further still, we come up with the common belief that this sort of charisma is caught rather than taught. 'You've either got or you have not, that certain thing . . .' as the song from 'The Desert Song' explains in connection with another sort of human attribute.

Secretly − or indeed openly − we all harbour admiration for the notion of the macho, granite jawed teacher of the past who supposedly froze children with a glance or, in extremis, felled them with one blow of his mighty fist. In dreams we see him, pacing a silent dining hall in which no child dares to refuse his cauliflower, and then going on in the afternoon to implant every single multiplication table into every single one of his class of sixty pausing twice only, once to eject a complaining parent from the classroom and once to be sarcastic to the inspector of schools.

In fact, of course, it never really was like that. The more brutal and screwed down the regime in the classroom the more likelihood there was of vandalism and the hurling of oaths or stones after teachers in the street – old school log books and genuine, as opposed to highly biassed, reminiscences demonstrate this beyond doubt.

This is not to say that authoritarianism never works at all. The point is that on the whole it only works when the people being disciplined have respect for those in charge. Even in the Army – perhaps the ultimate repository of traditional disciplinary methods – an infantry squad can make life hell for a junior officer who is held in contempt, notwithstanding the massive authority which lurks behind a lieutenant's badges of rank.

Where does this take us? I submit that it allows us to replace one over-simplification with another. School discipline is not about 'keeping order' in the sense of naked confrontation. What it is really about – and always has been – is winning cooperation, so that teacher and child can each see that the other is 'on our side'.

It would be foolish to suggest that confrontation never happens. What it does mean, though, is that if the general atmosphere is one of respect and co-operation, then such confrontations as do occur are far more likely to be defused and solved without general upset. Some children will always be disruptive; some teachers unable to cope. Safety and well-being will inevitably demand the application of rules and the devising of sanctions. 'Discipline', in other words, will always be an issue. The context, though, is vital, and will largely determine the frequency and seriousness of disciplinary disputes. We cannot, therefore, discuss discipline without discussing the whole of school life – indeed we may feel we need to discuss the way that society is put together. This constant tendency to digression bedevils all writing on discipline. Nevertheless, the authors of these papers have managed to keep the debate within bounds and on terms which are easily recognisable by the classroom teacher. The writers all tell us of their experiences as well as of their ideas. There is a wide and interesting spectrum of opinion on view and, let it be said, a variety of shades of optimism about what is possible in the school setting and what is not.

Each author has, of course, written about what he knows, and in every case what the author knows is of direct interest and utility to his fellow educationalists, especially if these latter are teachers or student teachers. Failures are presented with successes, because the old cliché about learning from failure is no less true for being overworked.

Inevitably, and indeed quite deliberately, the views expressed here cover a very wide spectrum. There are the so-called 'traditionalist' thoughts of Joseph Newman, for example, to set alongside the 'progressive' arguments of Richard Martin and Jenifer Smith. What strikes me, though, is not that there are unbridgeable gulfs or even startling contrasts. Instead, as I have read these papers I have come to view them as differing perspectives infused and inspired by similar basic elements.

Thus do I believe that it is what is *common* to these papers which is heartening and optimistic. Each writer is saying that schools can work; that formal education is necessary and important. Further, each writer is saying that the only hope of success lies in treating children as fellow human beings – that if we trample on their needs and feelings, we deserve all the disciplinary trouble we will inevitably get. The most important message which comes through – and authors must forgive me for so pre-empting it in this introduction – is that before, during and after discipline comes *caring*. The teacher who does not, or is not prepared to, care for his pupils does not need this book. What he needs is another sort of job!

We have come to take for granted the idea that traditional attitudes to authority have declined, and this is not, I think, something with which we can seriously argue. The 1960s, I suppose, will go down in the history books as the peak of the anti-authoritarian movement. It was the decade of mini-skirts, 'Swinging London' and the start of soccer hooliganism. In the sixties, students exchanged blazers and crew cuts for sweat shirts and anti-Vietnam-War placards. After all that, even given the assumption that there must be some sort of back-lash, some observers are, I think, surprised to find that there are schools which preserve, cherish and encourage in an explicit way such virtues as obedience, courtesy and the need to shut up and work.

It seems important to me, therefore, to start this collection of writings off with one which reminds us that authoritarian-ism is not, and never has been, dead. Throughout the progressive sixties, and on into the troubled seventies, a very large number of schools consistently and continuously proved every single day that they were open that it is still possible to run a school on traditional lines – provided always that rules were interpreted with compassion and that respect between teacher and pupil was not only earned but was always a two-way affair.

1

This first piece is by Joseph Newman, head of Matthew Arnold secondary school on the outskirts of Oxford. Joe Newman is the most committed schoolmaster I have ever known. He will forgive me, perhaps, if I suggest that his philosophy is basically a simple one, best summed up with the words authority and care. Joe believes that kids should behave themselves, listen to their teachers and do as they are told. If they fail to do this he is prepared to punish them, by beating if necessary.

At the same time he is a caring man, who would miss any number of meals and engagements so long as one of his pupils needed his help or his presence, and would assuredly take to task any teacher who through carelessness or deliberate injustice made a child unhappy. This kind of paternalism is, of course, old fashioned in that it presupposes a set of relationships which are less egalitarian than many people today would accept. That Joe still deeply believes in his way of doing things, and is prepared to be unpopular if necessary rather than bend to the wind, is a measure of his own strength.

It has become something of a cliché to say that progressive methods are hard work, with the concomitant implication that authoritarian methods are easy. What Joe Newman says here, and what I have observed of his work, gives the lie to this. Schoolmastering of any brand is extremely hard work if it is properly done.

Care and Authority in the Secondary School

JOSEPH NEWMAN

When I was eleven years old, my reverent hands received a brand-new copy of *Latin for Today*, Book I, and I have a memory of reading on line 1 'Discipuli, picturam spectate.' I cannot remember the picture, although I spectated it forthwith, but I do remember the blind glow of joy which I felt at learning that I was a *discipulus*. I think I was a very amenable *discipulus*, not to say creep, for I fell out with authority very rarely, and I soon discovered the necessary placatory behaviour for regaining approval on the few occasions on which I did. I was an only child, brought up in the country by elderly parents during the war, when all children were expected to conform, shut up and get on with it. Being clever and tolerably industrious, I did well in lessons and was frequently praised. I could not, and at first thought still cannot, understand those who go out of their way to dodge lessons, commit offences, or fail to work. Then, however, I recall Physics, Art and PE. I was a ham-fisted, clumsy fellow, and my opacity to Physics teaching was a byword. I try to guess what I might have been like if I had stumbled through lesson after lesson in all subjects with increasing incomprehension and irritation, as some children do. Would I have sought relief in crime or insubordination? I shall never know, for I have always been on the side of the good boys.

What is more, I sympathise with the good boys more and more as time goes on. Once upon a time, the young had original sin imputed to them. I might have found that interesting at least. It is the unoriginal sin that some youngster go in for that bores me so profoundly. So do many of the reasons which they have learnt to advance for their wickedness. I remember one lad of eleven who had done numerous burglaries and related offences. I asked why he did such things. He said it was because of the broken marriage. I asked if he meant his own. He looked uncertainly at me and then at the door; only a raging nutcase could ask such a damfool question. I pressed him to give me one cogent reason why the discomforts of his parents should impel him to breaking and entering. He could not answer. It would be comfortable to say that after this exchange he reformed and never climbed another drainpipe, but alas this is not so. Meanwhile, however, a large number of youngsters brought up by single parents behave well and many with the usual number of parents do not.

I think we can be too understanding. A bit of ferocity suitably applied can be very worthwhile. The majority of youngsters want to get their schoolwork done satisfactorily, learn their lessons, produce their art and drama and science, get their sums right, earn their qualifications, and so forth, without needless bother from the rest of the class. The majority do not steal, destroy, write on the wall, punch others on the nose, or smoke in the lavatories. Indeed, they want to be protected from all those who do such things. Everyone is happier if there are no disruptions of that kind. I think even the naughty ones would rather feel a firm control for the sake of the security it gives. I do not believe that many children really enjoy being naughty; it may give them some excitement, but it is an idle excitement, which they pursue *faute de mieux*.

Applicants for teaching posts, especially young ones, often ask me what our disciplinary system is. Upon enquiry I usually find that they really want to know what deterrents we have. They listen to my exposition of the matter with a kind of eager embarrassment; they often seem to want to have support and power of control, but they would like it to be external to themselves. Impositions, fatigues, detentions and corporal punishment all have their value, and if they are appropriate we should use them. I find it disconcerting as headmaster to be faced with threats of violence or of legal suit on the part of parents, with publication in the paper of a picture of a boy's backside with cane marks on it, with libels or slanders on the part of parents or their unions and so on. At the time one could be forgiven for wishing that one had dealt with the matter differently, but if the action was right in itself it remains right in spite of the threats. One's colleagues need one's support.

Over the entrance to Dante's Hell there was a notice saying that it had been made by God's love. After reading the details of the ingenious tortures within, we may wonder at this a bit, but Dante and many other theologians had no doubts. They saw the punishment of evil as the obverse of the reward of virtue. Society is curiously divided about corporal punishment. Many members of the public believe that it is now prohibited, and they long for its return as a sort of disciplinary panacea. I have seen a transfigured glory in the eyes of some of them when they learn that I still cane really naughty pupils, and I have felt quite embarrassed at their naiveté. They seem to think that a good thrashing ('It never did me any harm, Headmaster') is the answer to the whole delicate business. Most of these people are fifty or over, but not all of them are, and some are parents at their wits' end to know how to deal with their difficult teenage children. They come seeking an external solution too, and there is surely something Freudian in the way that some fathers say 'Capital punishment' when they mean 'corporal punishment'.

So colleagues, pupils, parents, and members of the general public are inclined to look to the school and the headteacher for support. This may quite easily go too far. Sometimes I am telephoned by people who have suffered some irritation or crime. They do not know who did it; they certainly do not know that our children are involved; and the event has not taken place in school time; but they see the headteacher as a combination of God, a cheap policeman who needs no evidence and need not keep to the law, and a definable object of complaint. I am sure that we must put a limit on the extent to which we accept this impossible role.

Nevertheless, we cannot completely limit ourselves to the school site and the period of 9 a.m. to 4 p.m. We are aiming to provide the most favourable, exciting, and comforting conditions for children to grow up in. We expect them to learn more than we did; to be more confident and mature; to speak well; to dress neatly; to be kind to each other; to play music, to produce art, and to act better than we did; to go to foreign countries and to take risks at games and outdoor pursuits. I could not have done many of the things that we ask our children to do, and it behoves us all to remember our own schooldays with cold accuracy and not through the golden haze of saloon-bar nostalgia. I once opened a package in my attic and found therein some of my school exercise books. Every teacher should undergo that experience. I was pretty shaken by the immaturity, the poor penmanship, the spelling errors, and the simplicity of the ideas – and I was one of the successful ones! We have to temper our demands for perfection with the knowledge that it is more likely to be approached than achieved.

On the other hand, we do have to pursue ideals rather than purely and immediately possible ends. We do have to keep trying to do better than before. Success in last year's exams is of no value to this year's candidates. I believe that children really do want to cooperate in learning, and that a fellow-feeling with their teachers is essential. It distresses me greatly when I hear that a child feels, however wrongly, that a teacher is being unjust or unkind. Also, I like to think that the teachers seek other contacts with the pupils (through societies and other out-of-school activities) than merely in the classroom. I would equally want all headteachers to teach, to prepare candidates for external exams, and to involve themselves in club activities. There must of course be a clearly defined system of pastoral care and proper opportunities for parents to confer with the school, but the root of success must be direct and personal. I think a pupil must care about his teacher's good opinion, and, wishing to gain it, he will try to succeed. We expect our pupils (and our colleagues too) to do more than they comfortably can, and they deserve the support of warm personal feeling. Smiles, greetings, and praise are the most essential disciplinary devices, and the last is the easiest to forget.

But enough of generalisation. What I will do now is try to list, under appropriate headings, some of the important issues surrounding the subject of discipline.

Physical provision: the environment of learning

Discipline is the proper condition for a pupil, for a disciple. It is a complex of facts, attitudes, and physical things. The books, tools, furniture, and other devices must be present when they are wanted; weak provision of those will exasperate everyone and destroy the children's faith. The buildings must be warm, convenient, attractive, and well decorated. Your caretaker is an essential ingredient in discipline, for he encourages the children to have a high regard for the actual fabric of the school. Flowers in the classrooms, seats in the grounds, neatly kept shrubs, and rugger posts in place when wanted are all important. The physical environment of learning is desperately important in the maintenance of morale. My own school went through a traumatic period when new temporary buildings could be reached only over a sea of mud, for we had no paths; heaps of builders' rubble abounded; and intended lawns and flower beds were indistinguishable from primal chaos. No children can function adequately in such conditions; discipline cannot be maintained.

One school in which I worked had apparently been designed by an architect who had met and contemplated real children in the mass. He had provided coved terrazzo floors with the walls tiled in various bright and pleasant colours up to shoulder height. The classroom walls had chairback rails on them, and the furnishings were of good quality. The next school that I went to had been designed for low capital cost; it never looked as exciting as it should, and the repair bills were wicked. Physical conditions in school are far more important than either the public or the county councillors realise.

The probationary teacher

One of a headmaster's commonest headaches is the probationer (or older teacher, for that matter) who cannot keep order. Parents write scathing letters of complaint, the children ask for transfers to other teachers, and colleagues approach one with embarrassed discretion. What can one do? Occasionally a punitive expedition may be called for, but its effect is ephemeral, however much the probationer may both fear and desire it. Advice may help, and most probationers get plenty of it, some of which they may scarcely comprehend. I remember the advice I was given. It went like this:

> HM   You're having trouble with IVB Latin, I believe.
>
> Self   Yes sir, I'm afraid I am a bit . . . er . . . it's like this. . . .
>
> HM   You're not paid to have trouble with IVB; you're paid to teach them.
>
> Self   Yes sir.

After this brief colloquy I felt pretty sour. The man was supposed to help me, I thought. I had supposed that headmasters were all-powerful men who could put such matters right in a second. Now that I *am* a headmaster, busy and sometimes harassed with a score of petty problems, I feel more sympathy for my former head. I was, after all, being paid £10 a week (less tax, superannuation etc.) to teach, and if I couldn't do it then I was obtaining money by false pretences. In fact, I returned to the fray and eventually I won, or, to put it another way, IVB became VB and decided that they had better get down to their work and have a go at their exams. In short, they joined me. That is quite often what happens, but time is a very slow healer and we are all impatient.

What *can* one do for the probationer who has disciplinary problems? We can visit him to see what is going wrong. We can look at his lesson notes, his marking, and so forth. There may be a hint in that. The main causes, however, are likely to be tiredness and fear. We experienced teachers are often tired, and yet we are probably getting a great deal more done than the probationer. His trouble is that he works inefficiently and uncertainly. The best thing that we can do is insist on his adopting simple aims and really fulfilling them, rather than labouring mightily to stimulate imagination and to entertain the unwilling. There's plenty of time for all that when the pupils are quiet enough to hear it. Also, the teacher who marks and prepares till 5 a.m. has precious little left to give at 9 a.m. that same day. We need to help keen, nervous young people who have only just finished with being university students to give up the anarchic sleeping and working habits that some of them follow. Finally, however, it may be necessary to be a bit ruthless and point out that they are paid to teach and not to groan and beat their brows like late nineteenth-century actors.

Supporting one's colleagues

Henry V saw that few kings could bring to battle an army consisting of all unspotted soldiers. We are in like case. We may find that some dinner lady, or lab technician, or teacher indeed, has taken a thoughtless action, found that it has failed, and then brought the whole sloppy mess to us to clear up. Dewlap trembling and eyes both flashing and tearful, he or she stands there accusing the wickedness of the young and implying the inadequacy of our disciplinary influence. Then what do we do, as resentment and exasperation creep up the backs of our minds and turn our smiles of goodwill into a grim rictus (until we remember to clear it away and look appropriately solemn)? Once upon a time, we would have sailed forth, gown flowing in the wind, and administered semi-justice with all ferocity. Perhaps we sometimes still do. I, however, am getting older; it won't be long before I am standing in front of another Judgement Seat, and a really omnipotent and omniscient voice will remind me of what I did unto one of these little children. Putting it another way, I am beginning to wish for more justice and less histrionics. Occasionally we *must* say 'I have doubts of your action in this matter. I will do my best to get you off the hook and establish a proper state of affairs, but I will break neither the law of the land nor the principles of justice.'

The the complainant goes back to the staff room and says that he doesn't know what the world is coming to, and one can't get the support from the Old Man that one is entitled to etc. etc. On such occasions do not bug the staff room; that way the screaming hab-dabs lie. It is better not to know.

Furthermore, if there is a general atmosphere of justice, kindness and firmness, the odd mistake soon dilutes itself into oblivion.

Classroom pests

What does one do about the truly disruptive class member, who swears at the teacher, refuses to work, is challengingly disobedient, and so on? These pupils are fairly rare, but they do occur, and they cannot be disregarded. Some of them are under dreadful pressures and need help desperately. They deserve help – but not toleration of such behaviour. I remember a lad who lost his temper with a prefect and thereupon kicked the window out of a fire-door. I caned him and told him that he would have to pay something towards the cost of repair. That evening he told his father, who flew into a rage at my injustice (as he saw it) in punishing the boy twice. The man then had a heart attack and died. The boy felt guilty and resentful. I tried to comfort him the next day. We had a number of disagreements over a substantial period, and then he went elsewhere for treatment. Soon after his return to school he took his exams and left. He took a job, succeeded at it, settled down, and is a substantial citizen – and always accosts me in a most friendly way. I recall feeling rather lonely that morning when he told me of his father's death, but I still believe I was right. There are people who make so many allowances for naughty children that they write off their guilt for their misdoings altogether. The world will not do this later on; the school cannot afford to do it now. We have to ask ourselves if the misbehaviour is straightforward naughtiness or if it indicates a need for specialist help. Specialist help does not always work, but we neglect it at our peril.

Remedial teachers in the nature of things find that they have most contact with the sort of difficulty that arises from a child's incompetence and expresses itself in outbursts. They have an extremely difficult course to set. If they apply draconian punishments every time, they will at the very least lose the pupil's trust. If they accept such outbursts as normal, they are doing the pupil and all his subsequent associates a disservice. Pupils of limited intelligence are often limited in emotional development too, and it may well be that in helping them to grow up in that sense the remedial teachers are doing a greater service than when they teach them to read, write, and reckon, important though those skills are.

The other pupils are a strong disciplinary force, if they wish to be and if they have the right standards. In serious matters they are inclined to severity, and we have to mitigate the effects of this. In lesser matters they can be sadly tolerant. Litter-dropping, graffiti-writing, and minor damage do irritate them, but schoolboy honour will discourage them from reporting the offenders. Sometimes in such cases a frontal attack is called for. If you are troubled with a stink-bomb-dropper, you may have to do as they did in the eighteenth century when troubled with uncatchable highwaymen, and threaten pretty dire punishment. Get that in writing, with a date on it. Then, if a victim *is* apprehended, do what you threatened, even if his father *was* the principal contributor to the music fund or the minibus project!

Parents

When reading some articles about indiscipline among school-children, one might be forgiven for taking it that children are as crocodiles were once thought to be – bred out of the mud by the operation of the sun. In fact, they have parents, and most of them have two each. On the face of it, furthermore, the parents and the schools would appear to have a community of interests: we all hope that the children will do well in all respects.

The great majority of parents are indeed most helpful, but such is human nature that we are more conscious of the difficult ones than their number warrants. Some parents, remembering their schooldays obscurely and self-defensively, see the teacher as a villain at the outset. It still amazes me when parents accuse us, in a near-falsetto caused by rising hysteria, of 'pickin' on me daughter' or of 'always getting on to *my* son when you don't say nothing to the others.' In such cases letter-writing is not always helpful, and I am not now making snide jokes about the ones who cannot read at all. Our careful jugglings with *mots justes* will get us nowhere with people who have only vague ideas of words. 'Immorality', for instance, has an inevitable and immediate sexual connotation for some people; 'impudent' and 'imprudent' might as well be the same word; and so forth. How are we to gain the help and cooperation of these people? It is often such parents who produce the children who cause trouble, so we need to find a way. Many of them live by gossip, so dark threats about suits for slander when they speak ill of our colleagues will merely puzzle them. They might as well be sued for coarse fishing or bingo, which are also hobbies.

If parents of this kind turn out stroppy, what is to be done? Above all, do not lose your cool or forget to wear your gown. Often their awkwardness arises from fear; let that fear ripen into respect. Never use any phrase that can be construed as objectionable, but let your pejorative terms be solemn and obscure. Then, more in sorrow than in anger, bring the conversation round to the thought that (provided we all work together and show goodwill) it is just possible that in the fullness of time you may be able to bring yourself to write little Johnny an employment reference. It will not have occurred to the parents that you might not have done this; the realisation can be salutary. Of course, I am assuming that it was little Johnny's ill-behaviour that precipitated the trouble. Otherwise, of course, to refuse a reference would be tyrannical. From there on, you may well be able to work *with* the parents for Johnny's good.

Not always, though. Even when they are on your side, they may not be able to help. Many parents really are at a loss to know what to do with their difficult children. They feel as if parental life is a sort of roller-coaster ride, and they prefer to hold on with both hands and shut both eyes, praying to whatever gods may be that their children will be off their hands before anything really dire occurs. Many of them, when the child has actually embarked on a life of utter indiscipline at home, or indeed of crime, can hardly credit that they have nourished such a viper in their bosom, and stand appalled at what they see. My heart aches for them, especially when they seem to believe that it is all easy for me and that I just need to wave my wand and all will be well. Probably, indeed, we teachers could do much, were we not so thin on the ground, and were we not actually appointed to teach History and Algebra.

Then there are the (usually better-off) parents who have tried everything and failed. Sometimes they come complaining about the quality of the teaching, but sometimes their children have kicked over the traces and they come speaking less forcefully and more in a spirit of entreaty. The young girl whom they cared for so well ('We've never refused her anything, Headmaster') has told mother where to put her washing-up and has responded to father's rebuke by flouncing out of the house and spending the night in a barn. Often there have been signs of difficulty in school too. Here we have to keep the child's belief in our love without giving the impression that we are soft in the head. 'What *am* I to do?' cries the parent, as if expecting to be given some 'Open Sesame' formula that will put everything in order. 'You talk to her, Headmaster,' they say, propitiatingly, 'She thinks so highly of you.'

'Does she, hell!' I think, as I smile in appreciation of their flattery; but at the same time I know that I must do something. Somewhere there is a road to this confused pupil's heart and common sense; can I find it between 0930 and 1005 on Monday? If not, I shall have to go and teach 5/7 and hope that she doesn't go off the boil for ever before I can get back to her.

Fortunately most parents are very sensible, and so are their children. They are often anxious, however, and demand instant retribution upon the pupils who disrupt their children's lessons, and upon the teacher who permits them to do so. Having been biddable enough themselves, and having often been taught in a grammar school of thirty years ago or other similar rather rarefied atmosphere, they think that it is mere laziness or perverseness on the teacher's part that accounts for X's presence in the classroom at all, quite apart from his aberrant behaviour. To counsel patience to such parents, to tell them to wait a couple of years before we civilise X, is of no avail. They want him bastinadoed now. And they *are* on our side! They have honoured us with a sacred trust in giving us the care of their children (and that is truth, not irony). They are confident that little Stephanie is making slow progress in Maths because of inexplicable mixed-ability teaching and noise. And they are partly right. Let us put our professional pride in our pockets, and cooperate with these good parents, even if they seem occasionally wrong-headed. One day Stephanie will be successful, or at the very least she will be happy and kind to her own children and a good citizen in her neighbourhood. From our bath-chairs we shall see it, and verily we shall have our reward.

When you want to enlist parental help to bring your Eric to heel; to stop him dipping the teachers' handbags; to discourage him from bopping opposing rugger players on the nose; to limit his intake of Southern Comfort during the lunch break;

or to hold him back from cattle rustling till he is really old enough, by all means ask his parents to come and see you, but at the same time remember that if they won't defend him then he is probably defenceless. Therefore, step firmly but thoughtfully across the quagmire of their natural suspicion. Wear a smile and an outstretched handshake. They probably do want to help but they need to be helped in order to help.

There is one sort of case which I find especially difficult. This is where, with good intentions but in haste or fatigue, we (or one of our colleagues responsible to us) have administered summary justice which is either of suspect validity or downright wrong. For ourselves it may be possible, but not easy, to admit error; for our colleague that might be dangerous. Pray hard, be unfailingly courteous, and play it by ear. Often the truth is complex, and no one is fully right. There is no simple answer, for most of us.

It was otherwise with a former headmaster of mine. There was a certain youth whom he frequently caned for various villainies. One day it came to pass that this youth was sent down to him to receive his meed of praise for doing a really good piece of work.

'What,' cried the Head, without a moment's enquiry, 'You again?' and gave him six. Only then did the lad's purpose in coming to him reveal itself. Even the Head was a little abashed, but he held his ground. He persuaded the lad that, on past form, he was bound to deserve at least ten strokes in the immediately ensuing months, and he struck a bargain to remit that number and not merely the six which had been improperly administered. They shook hands gravely and with expressions of mutual goodwill and parted at the study door. The credit balance of ten strokes seemed too valuable for the naughty lad to imperil, and he never returned to draw on it. Perhaps he had already decided to reform anyway. At the very least this serves to show that that particular Headmaster's dunghills always smelt of violets. Mind you, that doesn't apply to most of us. If we did that sort of thing, a parental neck-tie party would be outside the study windows in next to no time.

Let me say again, however, that most parents are helpful, sensible and supportive. I concentrate on less happy situations because they are the ones in which we need help and a sense of sympathy.

Up to now I have viewed the matter largely from the point of view of the Head, though I hope that it may be of use to other teachers to see things from that angle. Now perhaps I may be permitted to call on memory and observation and try to be helpful to classroom teachers and, in particular, the younger ones.

The difficult lesson

You go into class one day, soon after your arrival at your first school. You are firmly persuaded of the importance of matrices or the Treaty of Brest Litovsk or the reproductive cycle of the crayfish. Furthermore, you have checked a few of the more elusive details of your topic the night before. The class is a bit bubbly, the afternoon is warm and oppressive, the air is scented with wet raincoats, and it is Friday. After a shout or two from you, they fall moderately silent, however, and you begin. Then you notice X's attention fading. He pushes a piece of inky paper towards Y. Z giggles and nudges her neighbour. You glower; they fall temporarily silent; and you struggle on – but you have lost the hearts-and-minds battle. How do you proceed? No one has done anything that a court would take seriously, but Brest Litovsk is sadly out of focus.

I wish I could tell you of a simple foolproof answer, but there isn't one, except the bell at the end of the lesson. Try opening the windows wide; try a sudden test; even admit failure and ask the pupils what they would do; but never just fade. When you are new in this business, do whatever you do do crisply, even if you are wrong. In the actual classroom you can no longer afford the long meditations which lead toward absolute truth; get the whole numbers right and to hell with the decimals, at least until you are fully in charge.

Duty day

You are on duty and the weather is foul. Most lunches are over, and the school contains numerous bored and slightly uncomfortable teenagers. You are a woman of twenty-two, and you stand about five feet one inch in your umbrella. A prefect reports a bit of a fight in the social area. You can't see over the heads of the onlookers, so you blunder on till you reach the middle of things. Then what? Use the lower register of your voice; put in plenty of power; order the offenders to stand still in a given place; lecture the onlookers briefly; take two or three names, including at least one that you yourself know; and march the pugilists to someone in authority. Don't attempt to use force; you haven't got much, and it gains very little respect anyway.

For such events, the more names you know, the better. There is a sort of witch-doctory in a name, pronounced in ringing tones. Have names by you to strengthen your arm in this way.

Suppose, however, that your clear and ringing orders obtain no acknowledgement, or even some rude words and giggles and surreptitious pushes in the back. What then? Frankly, I'd look for another post forthwith. No one ought to accept such a situation, and no headteacher ought to draw his salary when such things occur. The Headmaster may be new, however, and keen to set things right. If that is so, he needs and deserves your support. Go to your head of department and see what can be done to raise a common agreement amongst the staff to exert a strong disciplinary effort. It must be consistent, continuous, and cooperative. Everyone must do all that he can and only pass the problem up the line if it is really beyond him. As soon as teachers start neglecting examples of serious indiscipline or merely complaining about the apparent inaction of senior staff, then the day is lost.

Prefects

The older pupils have had the advantage of being looked after when they were young; now they have the responsibility in turn of looking after the juniors. More and more I think that *all* sixth formers should do some duties for the young. What's more, these duties should be as wide as possible; helping with registration groups, hearing reading, and generally dealing with organisation of pupils outside class time. The clearer and more regular the disciplinary duties are, the better. We can expect sixteen and seventeen-year-olds to show some initiative, but we can also expect them to make some mistakes.

Therefore they need to be able to refer quickly to a teacher – any teacher. Some new teachers, aged about twenty-two, feel very young when under pressure, and turn very readily to seniors for help. Sometimes this is necessary, but by no means always. They should reflect that, thirty-five years or so ago, a young man of their years could easily have been out in the jungle or the desert in charge of a battery of twenty-five-pounders or high up in the air flying a Lancaster. When a decision was called for he had to make it and risk it, there and then. What's more, if he made an error he did not have Jimmy Smith's cheeky voice to deal with; he had a lot of unfriendly Germans or Japanese. That sort of thing concentrates the mind wonderfully.

Therefore, when you are on duty, be thorough, be decisive, and be supportive to your prefects. They'll help you in return, and the young will respect both you and them. A bit of thought about the duties and the mode of command appropriate to an officer would be of use to most schoolteachers. I realise that you aren't backed up with courts martial, firing squads, and such like. In effect an officer isn't either. We have far faster powers of summary justice than officers have; if we are ready to use them quickly, we shall have to use them rarely.

The School Rules

Once upon a time I was outraged (and enraged) at what seemed to me to be a gross instance of injustice on the part of my Headmaster. He had at first apparently passed over an action on the part of some boys and then later had punished them to support a new and rather wobbly Boarding House Master. The thing that worried me was that the boys might see injustice in his change of attitude. It was perhaps worse that in fact they seemed to accept it as a normal, typical piece of pedagogical double-think. I now see that the Headmaster was caught in a pincer situation: there was really no great wrong in what the boys did (they had been late back after giving their services as musicians at an Old Boys' Dinner Dance) but the headmaster had felt it necessary to stand up for the Housemaster, who got a bit hysterical at having to stay up till after midnight to count the lads in.

There are two things to learn from this. Next time you ask the Head to inflict condign punishment for chewing in class or for possibly having been one of those who said something rude, look at the wider issues. Secondly, do not expect any human institution to reflect absolute justice. Our own English laws and constitution are imperfect, after centuries of effort by lawyers and politicians specially trained for the job. Ergo, the School Rules, however neatly duplicated, will have great gaps in them, where common sense is the only bridge. Don't expect every eventuality to be covered. Be prepared to make a decision and stick to it, but when you do so remember that the Head will be in a weak position if what you decided to do is illegal by the laws of the land.

Be sure your own group or form know the rules; post them up on the notice board as required; and know them well enough to refer to them if you have to. If you decide that one of them is wrong, do not disregard or countermand it, but raise the matter at the staff meeting or other proper place, and get it changed if possible by the standard means.

When acting by the school rules, be firm but also try to recall that even smoking in the lavatories is not a capital offence or a deadly sin: really to lose one's temper with a child is undignified and a waste of precious nervous energy, though to appear to do so may be necessary at times. Even that piece of acting should be sparingly employed, or you will debase the coinage.

Your group

Most teachers have a form or group to care for. Do everything that is connected with them efficiently, such as reading out notices, making lists, keeping an eye on announcements that affect them, and so forth. If they need help or are in trouble, see that nothing in their favour goes by default. Let them care for you because you care for them.

Inevitably you will enter into their relationships, making and sharing jokes, knowing about Jackie's predilection for chocolate or Bill's fear of spiders, but never pushing things so far that either feels ashamed or resentful of your knowledge. They will form your power-base in the school. They will imbibe your standards (so make them good!). They will remember you in thirty years' time. Then, when one of them does something wrong, a cold blank look and a sorry word from you will wound like a whipping. That is a dreadful power to wield; wield it with love but without shrinking.

Promotion

Discipline is a basic part of our trade. If you develop skill in it, you may be the more likely to achieve promotion. In case you do, learn all you can from the successes and failures of your seniors. Maintain your sense of humour and your clear memory. Leave nostalgia for the evenings and weekends. Be firm with yourself: you will be a pretty wet disciplinarian if you neglect your preparation for lessons, omit your marking, or take a day off for inadequate cause. Discipline is even more difficult if you are not fully fit, I know, but in fact most children do make allowance for your laryngitis or whateverelseitis. New teachers are fair game for all the bacteria that their classes can offer: and when you are tired you will be particularly liable to catch, or fancy you have caught, some ailment. It is particularly luxurious to stay at home and let your colleagues earn your salary for you. Nevertheless, come to school if you can, laryngitis and all, and you may discover that silence in class really is a valuable disciplinary device. After all, the loudest and most continuous talker in class was you! Ssh! Let the customers think for themselves.

2

Joseph Newman's statement makes a good starting point, I think. For one thing it presents a picture of school life and school values which will be readily recognisable to most of us; the schools we went to, on the whole, were like that. What is important, and bears repetition, is that schools still are *like that, to a degree which might surprise many whose only information comes from the critics or from sensational press reports. What we must do now is seek out another sort of starting point, by looking at the way discipline is presented as an issue to teachers in training.*

Without any doubt at all, student teachers worry about disciplinary problems – if the worry is not there from the start, then the first teaching practice brings it on apace. This concern is paralleled by that of teachers in school about the preparation of students for the realities of classroom life. The feeling undoubtedly exists – even if it is not always expressed – that much of the time students spend on 'theory' might be a waste of time if the students cannot control their classes. Again, you see, the theme is: control, *then* teach.

The problem facing the college lecturer, though, is that while he may recognise the importance of discussing and even teaching 'class control', exactly how you do this in college is very difficult to see. For a lecturer to try describing the myriad exquisite nuances which surface in any lesson, under the general heading of 'order' or 'control' is about as realistic as trying to coach a football team without ever leaving the lecture room.

To say that every student does teaching practice, and this is when class control should be taught, does not really answer the problem. Teaching practice, after all, is short, and the demands on time within it are legion. In teaching practice the student must, *willy nilly, exercise a variety of teaching skills and if he is to do so then massive disciplinary problems must be dealt with by 'artificial' means – a change of class, close teacher supervision, even a change of school. It is a truism, also, that teaching practice is an artificial situation in itself. Generations of students have comforted themselves with the notion that 'all students are fair game', and that this explains much of their disciplinary ineffectiveness. This may or may not be true, but it is certain that the student can never be perceived as a* bona fide *full-time member of staff, part of the establishment.*

Given all of this, it is hardly surprising that students come away from college feeling ill prepared for life at the sharp end of the chalk. Dick Mills, the author of the next piece, is a senior lecturer at a college of education, and is totally mindful of all the problems which I have just laid out. How he himself defines them, and how he deals with them is instructive.

Class Control on Teaching Practice

RICHARD MILLS

'VD blinds; TP kills.' Not a universal sentiment, perhaps, but the feelings of at least one graffiti artist, weighing succinctly the comparative dangers of two horrors. Teaching practice wins hands down as the ultimate deterrent, not only on account of the physical effort, hard work and mental strain involved – all of which are, to the conscientious student, considerable – but also because of the nagging question, 'Who rules, OK?' It is a natural and proper anxiety, shared by all students in training, and in this two-part article I want to explore some of the ways in which such fears about ability to maintain discipline in the classroom may be reduced to an acceptable level, sufficient to sustain alertness but not leading to paralysis. Even the most experienced actor's performance will be heightened by a measure of anxiety.

In college

The graffiti sentiment is not, of course, a genuine *cri de coeur*, but rather the expression of a college in-joke, a restricted code statement of community solidarity, such as will be found in many a staff room. Within the security of the lecture or seminar room it is deceptively easy to explore, with objective detachment and cool reason, a disciplinary issue or encounter which, in the classroom, would have the heart and head racing. It is a danger which, in my view, should be brought into the open straightaway in college, not only to avoid otherwise inevitable loss of credibility but, more important, to establish the kind of frank and honest atmosphere in which students and lecturer will be able to voice their uncertainties in, and with, confidence.

A lecture on group dynamics, maladjustment, behaviour

modification, spiced with anecdotes in the Lecturer As Hero tradition, may be helpful, but I doubt it, although aspects of all these areas will be useful in other contexts, such as group discussion. What seems to me to be a more profitable approach, initially, is an exploration of students' own fears and beliefs about discipline. It is the beginning, in curriculum terms, of a situation analysis, and to this end I require third-year students to write briefly about their views, in the light of their second-year Teaching Practice experience. These notes from my present group are in front of me at this moment and they make interesting reading, revealing, as they do, major points such as the following:

(1) Differing approaches to discipline within one school, with half the staff adopting informal methods and a friendly approach, and the others maintaining a tight rein and a rigidly judgmental atmosphere. For our present purposes, it does not matter how accurate this student's perception was about that particular school. She has identified a contradiction which most experienced teachers would recognise in some degree. Which approach does the student follow? How does she develop her own personal and professional style? What noise level does she permit?

(2) Differing sanctions, stretching along a continuum of: raising of eyebrows; verbal rebuke; lines; extra work; withdrawal of privileges; detentions; corporal (almost capital) punishment. In some schools the class teacher is required to deal with all matters himself. In others, there is an elaborate hierarchical structure for relaying various offenders to the appropriate member of staff, rather like pigeon-holing letters at the postal sorting office. This is by no means the panacea some might think, although it can give temporary relief. Students (and teachers) complain that the senior member of staff either does nothing effective, or acts far too harshly. Perhaps the buck should, generally, stop where it starts – in the classroom. However, faced with variations in attitude, how does a student quickly learn the prevailing code of sanctions? If he asks about them too tactlessly on a preliminary visit prior to the start of Teaching Practice, he could convey either an indecent haste to inflict retribution, or a fearful lack

of confidence, from the start. For example, one final-year student, Peter, writes: *I was delighted that we were NOT told what we were supposed to do when discipline problems arose, because each one involves different pupils, with different needs and reasons for misbehaving.*

(3) Differing practices in terms of classroom ritual and management. Some classes line up outside the doors; others walk right in. Some classes stand when a visitor enters the room; others carry on working. Some sit in solemn ranks; others in small groups. Some are dismissed *en bloc*; others row by row. Some teachers distribute art/woodwork/science equipment themselves; others leave it to volunteers. A student teacher of a minority subject in secondary school, such as RE or Music, may well teach hundreds of children a week, previously taught by a variety of teachers. How does the student build on the norms established by the experienced teachers (assuming they are successful) and also develop an individual style? *In trying to move a little away from complete reliance on textbooks,* writes Pauline, *I ran into immediate problems. Children began running around the room, throwing chalk and shouting at one another. The only way I found in which I had any success in achieving my aims in an orderly fashion was by presenting the children with printed duplicated sheets of work, which I hoped would encourage them to write down their ideas.* This student has early learned the pessimistic, but often effective, strategy of containment by worksheet.

(4) Differing attitudes towards curriculum planning, ranging from the teacher who has a strict syllabus to be followed as inexorably as a train time-table, to the teacher who says, *Do what you like.* Neither extreme is welcomed by most students. There are, moreover, teachers who issue up-to-date stock lists, with details of book and non-book materials, audio visual aids, reprographic facilities, explaining school procedures for their use. There are others who disguise their possession of equipment of any kind more skilfully than Scrooge. Students have check lists of jobs to do on preliminary visits, such as scrutiny of stock and familiarisation with the building. Knowing your way around, in all respects, is an enormous aid to good discipline. How does the student cope in a secondary school department where administration is poor and procedures slack, or in a primary school where the Headteacher guards

the books as if the stock cupboard were part of a nuclear reprocessing plant?

(5) Differing perceptions of the status of student teachers. There is still the occasional school which does not admit students to the staffroom. In others they become virtually full members of staff, with access to staff and department meetings and the same power and authority, if not salary, as anyone else. Clearly, the student needs to know where he stands, and to what extent he will be supported by the power of the institution. As Helen complains: *Within the class there were several pupils I felt I could not control. I did not feel I had any resources to fall back on. It was as if the pupils knew there was a limit to what I could do.*

(6) Differing degrees of information about potential sources of trouble. Many teachers feel they are acting in the student's best interests when they identify every problem pupil in each class before the student takes over. Equally, many students, I have found, prefer to learn from their own experience (which might be very different from the teacher's) and to approach classes with an open mind, avoiding the labels which have been previously acquired. Another kind of dichotomy is expressed by Alan when he writes: *Useful guidance came from the teacher who gave me a run-down of the method he used on each kid. But I found that I needed to find my own approach, not to use his.*

Such are some of the common areas in which students experience difficulty in their practice schools. Bear in mind that what I have written is from the student's viewpoint. Seen from the experienced teacher's perspective, everything is so very different. He knows the system; his colleagues and his pupils; the chain of command within the institution. He has established his own rituals and techniques. He knows what he wants to do and is only occasionally thwarted by a difficult pupil or a tricky class. Hence, he needs to be extraordinarily sensitive and perceptive if he is fully to appreciate the student's difficulties.

Once these difficulties, then, have been identified and discussed in college, how may one proceed?

The first answer lies, I think, in the area of curriculum planning. The teacher who provides for his class plenty of appropriate and relevant material and differing experiences,

ensuring that all children can become involved and achieve
some success, gets off to a cracking start. To this end, a student needs to be guided by college and school in his preliminary visits, prior to Teaching Practice, so that, by the time his
practice starts, he will be familiar with the geography of the
building; with hardware and software; with the prevailing
ethos and attitudes; with the rituals of procedure; with something of the hidden curriculum of the institution. Above all, he
will have observed a good number of lessons and made notes
on them, either according to some pre-determined 'Schedule
of Things to Look For', or on a more intuitive basis. He will
have seen the class or classes he is to teach and discussed their
previous work with their teachers. He will have planned his
teaching scheme with advice from teachers and tutors so that,
when he comes to devise detailed lesson plans, they will be
appropriate and effective.

All this is an ideal. In real life there are many false starts or
culs-de-sac. Lesson plans which would delight a curriculum
planner's heart and have a clear sequence of Situation
Analysis, Aims and Objectives, Content, Method, Evaluation,
may fail miserably in execution for a variety of reasons. So the
student, who needs to have done all his homework in this
respect and be well prepared, needs also a certain emotional
detachment from his schemes, lest they act like an albatross,
rather than a life-jacket, as he enters the water. He needs to
know when to hold on and when to let go, and that only comes
with experience. In this respect, the junior or middle school
student should be better placed than his colleague in secondary school, since one class is easier to get to know than many
classes. Planning school work of any kind, back in college, is
an odd, but necessary, activity. It's rather like packing your
suitcase to travel to a little known country. Advisers can and
do help, but you need to buy extra or alternative items when
you arrive and meet the natives and experience the climate.
Some items, which you have carefully packed, turn out to be
so much lumber.

A second answer may be found in material *about* school. To
pursue the travel analogy for a moment: you can read books
and see films about residence abroad before you go. Perhaps
the actual country you are visiting won't be featured, but you

may pick up some useful tips. Let me be more specific.

Films made in and of school can provide very useful data for discussion in college. Students are not directly involved and can remain objective. In golf terms, they may improve their own game, by watching some shots by regular players, dealing with bunkers and all. Many professional films of school life appear idealised and unreal. But not all, and two films made of life in London comprehensive schools perhaps go to the other extreme in presenting a raw harsh world. I am referring to *The Best Days*? a BBC Panorama film of life in Michael Faraday school, March 1977. More relevant for our present purposes, since it is available for hire, either from Concord Films Council Ltd (201 Felixstowe Road, Ipswich, Suffolk IP3 9BJ) or from BBC Enterprises (Villiers House, The Broadway, London W5 2PA), is the film *School* in the *Space Between Words* series. This is a 55 minute, black and white film, made in 1971, and shows Maggie Dobson, Head of the English Department at Acland Burley comprehensive school, trying valiantly to cope with recalcitrant fourth-year boys and girls at the beginning of term. Comments from an American researcher, Dr Richard Suchman, are interspersed between shots of English lessons, staff discussions, administration meetings.

Scrutiny of lesson transcripts and teacher talk is a device which will sharpen the student's awareness of classroom language and interaction. *Space Between Words* contains a sequence which has now become quite famous as an example of how logic and good sense in spoken utterances are not necessarily a prerequisite for gaining and sustaining children's attention. Confidence, physical stance, status, context, are all significant. In other words, *how* you say something in front of children may be as crucial, or more crucial, than *what* you say. Students should at least be aware of this, even though they may not actually be taught to speak nonsense. Here is Mrs Fisher, Deputy Head, standing on the platform at assembly, addressing the whole school, maintaining good order while violating the laws of rational argument:

I'm sorry, everybody, but Mr Attey said 'No talking.' Now stand still. Everybody. (Pause). If we expect an absolute

standard we must have it, and those of you who have been
here before know . . . that we can easily afford to chop off
some time from some lessons, but we are going to have what
we want. So will you all take your own decision, now, this
minute, if you're going to do exactly as you were told.
(Pause). Somebody's not waiting properly.

It is a text which is rich in discussion possibilities.

These two films, *Space Between Words* and *The Best Days?*,
each of which is far from being a simple success story, have a
compulsive viewing quality and provoke a good deal of sensible and constructive comment about how problems might be
resolved. As any Teaching Practice tutor knows, it is easy to
give other people excellent advice, and it is good for the students to be allowed this luxury at times.

More immediate, in another sense, are college-produced
films and videotape recordings of students and/or tutors and/
or teachers in neighbouring schools. These films may be made
with specific objectives, such as the practice of opening and
closing lessons, as in a micro-teaching manner (see E. Stones
and S. Morris, *Teaching Practice: Problems and Perspectives*,
Methuen, 1972), where a particular skill is isolated for special
attention. Or they may be more all-embracing in trying to
capture the essence of a whole lesson. In either event, they
provide external data, which students may scrutinise and discuss within the security of their own setting, and without the
fear of personal assessment which, for many of them, is a
powerful and inhibiting force.

Similar data may also be provided by prose writing, of the
pedagogic, autobiographical and fictional kind.

Three books in the pedagogic category come to mind. *The
Craft of the Classroom* by M. Marland (Heinemann, 1975) is
packed with sound, if at times pedantic, advice on management and control, and has something to say to all teachers.
One headteacher of my acquaintance, a little misled by the
title, mistakenly sent it to her Head of Woodwork as a specialist craft text.

Louis Cohen and Lawrence Manion's book, *A Guide to
Teaching Practice* (Methuen, 1977), has a useful section on
'Control and Discipline' (p. 175f.) and offers a range of poten-

tially successful ploys to meet most occasions, each based on research evidence.

Class Management and Control, a Teaching Practice Workbook as part of a Teacher Education Project being developed at Nottingham University by E. C. Wragg (since moved to Exeter) *et al* (1977) is useful too. It consists of a series of evaluation questionnaires to be completed by the student and/or a fellow student and/or tutor and/or teacher. Each questionnaire focuses on a different teaching area and the evaluation is intended to sharpen a student's perception of his performance, either by self criticism or by comment upon a colleague. The areas covered are as follows:

Focus 1: Organising a Class
Focus 2: Vigilance
Focus 3: Developing Management Skills
Focus 4: Developing Relationships
Focus 5: Handling Individual and Group Work
Focus 6: Handling Difficult Classes
Focus 7: Sharpening Class Management Skills
Focus 8: Evaluating and Developing Your Own Teaching Skills.

In the autobiographical category, extracts from A. S. Neil's *Summerhill* (Penguin) and Edward Blishen's *The School That I'd Like* (Penguin), can be guaranteed to provoke most students. A more recent book, which is particularly helpful, is *The First Year of Teaching* by Charles Hannam *et al* (Penguin, 1976). This consists of a series of extended comments, often based on tape-recorded conversations, by primary and secondary school teachers in their first year as probationer teachers. It succeeds as a stimulus to discussion, partly because of the easy identification between contributor and student-reader, and partly on account of the graphic honesty of the accounts. Witness the predicament of Graham, a Geography teacher in a West Midlands comprehensive school:

Every now and then there were odd moments of unexpected success in the classroom but I battled with this fourth form, I really did battle. I can't say I acted reasonably all the time. In fact, on one occasion I just left the classroom, I mean they'd beaten me, and I skulked in the toilet and cried for about half a minute, having got a house tutor to take over.

To know that he is not alone is good therapy for the student-reader. Feeling isolated is devastating, as Jean, a junior school teacher in the South East of England, reports:

I had a very awkward teacher at one time next to me who used to come up when there was the slightest noise and say, 'I can't hear myself talk down there, could you shut your class up?' and I couldn't always shut my class up, so it was creating rather an awful situation. She never showed me how to do it. I had some friendly tips, I suppose, but they seemed to take it terribly light-heartedly and make jokes about it. Perhaps they didn't really understand how badly I felt about it. But I think it was awkward for the teachers too, because they don't like to approach us and say, 'Do you want some help? Can I help you?' They think they might be interfering. I really don't know why. Something to do with the professionalism.

How this highlights the case for good induction training.

The First Year of Teaching is written from the beginning teacher's point of view. A booklet which manages to combine awareness of teaching problems with understanding of pupil difficulties also is that compiled by Arfon Jones and Robert Forrest, entitled *A Continuing Approach* (1977). This is about the experiences of Group Four, 4 full-time staff, 1 part-timer and 45 inadequate and/or disruptive pupils from the third, fourth and fifth years of Sidney Stringer Community Comprehensive School, Coventry. Case studies of awkward pupils are particularly illuminating. These give the family history, personal background and academic attainment of individual young people, with information about the attention they receive in Group Four. In each case, this attention and treatment is based upon appropriate aims such as:

– improvement of attendance;

– exposure to a consistent and supportive environment;
– boosting of confidence and improvement of self-image;
– provision of intensive remedial help, particularly for
  language handicaps;
– preparation for a working life.

The point about all this is not that the student teacher will be
able to operate on Teaching Practice as do the staff of Group
Four; he would not have the time, nor the expertise. But in
reading and discussing such case studies, he should develop
some understanding of how a committed school sets about the
long-term professional business of trying to solve some highly
intractable problems and help some very difficult adolescents.
In this task the school does all it can in adapting itself to the
individual and, most important for credibility, it reports its
failures as well as its successes.

So much, then, for some of the pedagogical and autobiographical writing which may be used. Every reader of these
pages will be able to add his own materials to those mentioned
here. As for fictional writing, the field is enormous and, again,
only a small selection can be given from among the many
possibilities. The intention, let us remember, is to focus on
difficulties, disciplinary problems, potential confrontations,
and care should be taken to avoid the impression that there is
nothing more to school life than latent or overt hostility. In
fact, there is a danger in writing or talking about 'discipline'
(as opposed to 'pastoral care', which is a much warmer and
wider concept, or, more positive still, 'developing good relationships'). One's heart gets heavier and heavier as the
catalogue of problems rolls on inexorably. It is analogous to
the creeping melancholy which descends, with the Armistice
Day poppies, from the Albert Hall ceiling, first a trickle, then
a downpour. So the danger must be recognised and a balance
maintained.

Moreover, as it is fiction we are now considering, extracts or
poems should be used, not as case studies of real situations,
but as springboards for students' own experience. The following may be helpful in this respect:

Poetry

J. Beckett, *The Keen Edge* (an anthology of adolescent free verse), Blackie, 1965. Poems 7, 82, 88.

D. J. Enright, 'Blue Umbrellas' in G. Summerfield, *Voices 3*, Penguin.

P. Hesketh, 'Truant' in A. Rowe and P. Emmens, *English Through Experience* Book II, Blond, 1st edition, p. 190.

D. H. Lawrence, 'Last Lesson of the Afternoon' in A. Cattell and H. Gardiner, *Outlook*, Harrap, p. 76.

J. Prévert, 'Exercise Book' in R. Mansfield, *Everyman Will Shout*, OUP, p. 11.

V. Scannell, 'Schoolroom on a Wet Afternoon', *Outlook*, p. 75.

E. Smith, 'The Lesson', in *English Through Experience* Book V, p. 92.

S. Spender, 'My Parents Kept Me from Children who were Rough', on p. 43 of *Things being Various*, by S. Clements *et al*, OUP.

Y. Yevtushenko, 'Schoolmaster', *Everyman Will Shout*, p. 13.

Plays

G. Cooper, *Unman, Wittering and Zigo*, Macmillan Dramascript.

B. Hines, 'Speech Day,' in *The Pressures of Life*, ed. M. Marland, Longman Imprint series.

J. Mortimer, 'David and Broccoli,' in *The Personal Conflict*, ed. J. Hodgson, Methuen.

P. Nichols, opening monologue of *A Day in the Death of Joe Egg*, Faber.

Prose

J. Barlow, *Term of Trial*, Penguin, ch. 2.

E. Blishen, *Roaring Boys*, Panther.

M. Croft, *Spare the Rod*, Longman.

C. Dickens, *Hard Times*, Penguin, ch. 2.

B. Hines, *A Kestrel for a Knave*, Penguin.

A. Huxley, *Brave New World*, Penguin, ch. 2.

J. Joyce, *Portrait of the Artist as a Young Man*, Penguin, Part 1.

D. H. Lawrence, *The Rainbow*, Penguin, ch. 13.

D. Storey, *Saville*, Penguin, ch. 11.

In school

I have so far briefly considered some of the approaches which
might be adopted in college, given the constraints of time and
course structure. The intention is to give students the kind of
general training and background information which might
establish, to put it no higher, a disposition towards approach-
ing problems reasonably and in a mature manner. The solution of a particular issue can only be effected, if at all, when it
is encountered in reality, and when its urgency is so pressing
that some solution must be found. The student in the classroom is now the lone pilot in flight, facing an emergency, no
longer able to rely on the simulator, as he did in training, or
the co-pilot by his side. He may dimly be aware that he will be
a better pilot after a thousand hours flying time, but the
emergency is upon him now and it must be dealt with.
Moreover, he must survive.

Here there can be no substitute for substantial and sus-
tained school experience, and any student going into school
should be aware that the greatest potential source of help and
advice is the teacher in school, not the tutor in college. Ideally,
there will be a partnership of interest, and many recent experiments in teacher training (e.g. Pat Ashton's at the Open
University, from 1978 onwards) presuppose a group practice,
with one teacher, one tutor and four or five students all working together on matters of common concern. My own college
operates in this way with first-year students in primary
schools, and the system has improved each year as teachers
and tutors have got to know each other better and broken
down the mythical and real barriers which previously divided
them.

More often, however, the student is alone in a school, visited by his tutor no more than twice a week, and more probably once. Discussion of lessons and problems may take place
immediately after the observation if circumstances permit.
This has the advantage of immediacy, but is not necessarily
ideal. A period of reflection may be better, with a tutorial back
in college. In either event, the tutor will write a memo for the
student (retaining a copy for his own records) and place it in
the student's file. Such a memo may often appear to the student like the utterances of the Oracle at Delphi – incontrovert-

ible pronouncements of great moment. I don't suppose there are many tutors who regard them in this light, despite the *deus-ex-machina* quality of a tutor's intervention, particularly if he is dashing off to see another student. When using the word 'intervention', incidentally, I merely mean his presence in the classroom. This should, in my view, be as unobtrusive as possible. A tutor should not dream of indulging his ego by taking over the lesson from the student, unless positively invited to do so.

What he writes in his lesson criticism, especially about disciplinary problems, should be the kind of thing that a sensible experienced teacher would also say, although probably with greater specificity, since the teacher would know the situation so much better. In order to demythologise the lesson criticism still further, I will quote from some of my own recent comments to students in secondary schools, and risk the ridicule of present practitioners. Bear in mind the selective nature of this sample. The comments quoted relate only to matters of discipline and classroom management and they should be seen in the context of other advice about teaching method and content.

There seem to be at least three major areas which need constant attention: Class management and disciplinary ploys; Development of relationships; Teaching style.

Class management and disciplinary ploys

(1) To Raymond with eleven-year-olds for drama:

Your reading in this drama lesson clearly went well and the children were interested in the story. The key problem seems to be how to calm them down and get them pointing in the right direction. A few ideas here:
  (a) Clearly establish a ritual for gaining attention e.g. clapping hands; shaking tambourine; banging a drum; even blowing a whistle.
  (b) When you have attention, hold it for a few seconds before you say anything. Then speak quietly.
  (c) Think about the possibility of using slow motion movement. It's very difficult for the pupils to move very, very slowly *and* make a great noise.

  (d) Look at: *Teaching Drama* by R. Pemberton-Billing and J.
       Clegg, ULP, and *100 + Ideas for Drama*, A. Scher and C.
       Verrall, Heinemann.

  (2) To Stephen teaching Maths to twelve-year-olds:

Re discipline. Here are a few ploys:
  (a) *Ignore* (and continue to ignore) anyone who calls out.
      Eventually, all will get the message that the only way to
      get a response from you is to put up their hands.
  (b) Stand still, four-square at the front, when giving instruc-
      tions or information. Try not to wander at such times; it
      gives an impression of weakness.
  (c) Be prepared to wait for quiet and attention. Often a
      staring, pointed silence (i.e. you standing looking at the
      group, possibly with arms folded) is effective.
  (d) When you've got attention, speak much more quietly and
      this might have the effect of quietening down the class.
  (e) The group of four boys (stage right) is an extremely
      tricky one to handle. Have a word with Mr Jackson and
      think about the possibility of splitting them up. I think,
      too, that specific individual threats might work. I'm sure
      that many members of staff will have trouble with them.
  (f) Please arrange a time with me back in college to discuss
      these matters and don't get too depressed by the prob-
      lems of today's lesson. I'm fairly certain that substantial
      progress can be made.

  (3) To Mary, with a group of thirteen-year-olds for Social
Studies:

Individually, these children are splendid, as I think you
realise. They respond to help and appreciate it. Collec-
tively, they are difficult. There are thirty-three of them;
they're fairly uninhibited; and the structure of the room
(i.e. a long rectangle of table tops) poses problems. Have a
word with Mr Tate about this; you may be able to re-group
tables and children. One problem is that any visual aid on
the board has to be enormous if it is to be seen at the other
end of the room.

I suggest you get to know the names of the children as soon as you can, otherwise you're at a distinct disadvantage. One way of doing this is to swot up the class list before the lesson, and then practise recognition as you hand back homework.

(4) To Anne, with a fifth-year group for Careers:

Clearly a difficult group for obvious reasons: lack of motivation; lack of a sense of organisation or structure; general immaturity; probably a sense of failure. Are they leaving in three weeks' time?

Given these problems (and, no doubt, others I haven't stated) I feel that you did well to keep your temper, remain calm, focus their attention on the task and get them to do some work. The quality of the interview simulations improved as it progressed, and there were positive things to build on. Apart from anything else, the tape recorder can act as a useful disciplinary aid, and you used it quite successfully in this capacity.

The long-term answer (which can't apply to you with this particular group) is to get interested in their lives, backgrounds, hobbies and opinions. It's the obvious thing to say, of course, but it does pay dividends.

Development of relationships

(1) To Judith, with a first-year remedial group:

Your file is developing into a useful working document. I notice that in your evaluations you are still tending to think in terms of 'the group'. A phrase you often use is 'the pupils'. This is understandable at this stage but try to think more specifically in terms of the strengths and weaknesses, attitudes and ways of working of individual children. It's a counsel of perfection, but the aim is to become more and more aware of the needs of *all* your pupils, rather than the blanket response overall of the whole class.

(2) To Maria, with a third-year remedial English group:

Are you afraid of these boys or were you merely embarrassed by my presence? My advice to you is to *keep calm*, if you possibly can. Remain firm, of course, but don't get hostile. If you do, then the boys may respond by becoming hostile too. At present they are merely disorganised, lacking in discipline and testingly racialist.

Try not to shout, particularly in such a small room. Instead, go round working with each individual and treating each one as a reasonable person (some may even become so then!) One containment method is to keep them well occupied with work.

We will arrange to talk further back in College.

(3) To Celia, teaching third-year English:

Be careful. You're in danger of making the same mistake as on your previous practice – i.e. being too matey too early. You need at this stage a more professional stance. Try to cut out the little asides (e.g. 'My hero . . .' 'Don't worry . . .') They're acceptable from a firmly established teacher but I sense that you are trying to gain affection and friendship too cheaply. Such desirable rapport needs to be earned. I am fairly sure that these children will take advantage of your good nature if you allow them to (e.g. to begin with, the number of asides and increasingly rude comments will grow).

Teaching style

(1) To Peter, teaching second-year RE:

You need to develop a more stable, equable teaching style. At present you appear to crack a joke one moment and then threaten some kind of retribution the next. Children need consistency of attitude (and this is not equated with dullness). I suggest you leave a tape recorder running for your next lesson and you may pick up what I mean here in listening to it in the evening.

(2) To Morgan, with a second-year History class:

Good voice and rapport. When speaking to the whole group I suggest you stand up straight, with hands out of pockets, and ensure you are addressing the whole class (in the manner of a radar scanner) rather than directing most of what you say towards the window.

(3) To Paul, with eleven-year-old Geographers:

Another word of warning – again, not a major thing at this stage, but something to guard against. I can now see incipient signs of certain idiosyncratic verbal and physical gestures (e.g. looking over your specs at the pupils; intonation expressing incredulity or bewilderment etc.) which I suggest you try to avoid. We all have certain mannerisms which are characteristic of us, and that can't (indeed, shouldn't) be avoided, *provided* those mannerisms don't reach the level of caricature. That is the danger, so please be wary of it. It's interesting that such features weren't evident in your last lesson, but they were in this one. Ask me about this and I'll explain further.

All the foregoing comments, as all kinds of teaching, are based upon some theory, but they do not begin with theory. On the contrary, they begin from the pragmatic standpoint of what I think will work in that classroom with that student, without doing violence to one's own, or one's students', sensibilities.

Occasional shouting and class confrontation is not ruled out, provided it is going to be successful. Much better is the one-to-one confrontation *after* the lesson, or during breaktime, when there is no audience for the trial of strength. Like all good punters, you need to pick your winners carefully, after studying the form. You need to know what to ignore and successful selective blindness comes only with experience. Better than any confrontation is a more subtle approach, in the attempt to establish rapport between class and student teacher. The ultimate aim and key to the whole enterprise is the establishment of good relationships. Without such a network school may become prison. However, I do not believe one can, or should, deny the authority of the teacher; we are in an authority profession. But many a good leader leads either

48 Class Control on Teaching Practice

from the back of the column or, perhaps better still, the middle. He and his troops are travelling the same road and on the same side, as the title of this book suggests. Most troops are reasonable, if their leaders are known to be sensible and fair.

When teachers I am working with read such comments as quoted earlier, they appear to be unimpressed. That is comforting. For them to be astonished would suggest either brilliance beyond their comprehension or nonsense beneath contempt. The comments are, I hope, such as they would make themselves, and I should be pleased if more teachers would feel easy about offering constructive advice to students in the form of a written comment. Some, of course, give constant help day after day, in the way of background information, suggestions for future action, and discussion of lessons observed. But often they are unwilling to commit themselves on paper. They see themselves, rightly, as on the side of the student teacher and cannot sustain a judgmental role in a one-to-one situation. When severe comments need to be made they are often mediated through the tutor, who acts as a kind of trouble shooter, trying to bring management and the workers more closely together. It's an interesting role, and adds spice to any Teaching Practice. But it would be better if relationships between teacher and student and tutor were such that anything genuinely felt could be openly stated, and sometimes that does happen. Certainly, students like to know where they stand, and the bald phrase, 'That lesson was OK' is as unsatisfying as it is kindly meant.

Occasionally, with a really difficult group or problem pupil, the tutor is not convinced that anything he suggests will be effective. I think he should say so. Better to admit defeat than peddle fake medicine. If the teacher or deputy head cannot then propose a way forward, the student and the group may need to be separated and, in extreme cases, the student withdrawn from the school.

In very rare instances, a student needs to be withdrawn, either because the staffroom atmosphere is not sufficiently sympathetic to students in training, or because a personality clash renders the position intolerable. On one occasion, a sensitive and conscientious student of mine, having difficulty with two of his secondary school classes, had put down a newspaper cutting he had prepared, just before using it in a lesson, and the teacher sitting next to him in the staffroom set fire to it. There was general hilarity from other staff present, and the comment, 'That's ruined your lesson plan now.' The newspaper article was about violence.

One further point is worth stressing. A tutor may dispense good advice with the extravagance of a generous football pools winner, but the student may be unable to use this advice to good effect. The tutor, while trying other strategies, may find it easier to be patient than the class teacher whose pupils are being adversely affected. In this instance, the strength of relationship between school and college may be tested almost to breaking point. If the title of this book implies that pupils and teachers should be pulling together, then teachers and tutors should be similarly allied. This seems easier to effect at infant and junior stages than at secondary level, probably because one class, one student, one class teacher and one tutor can get to know each other more quickly and more deeply than hundreds of children and many different specialist teachers.

Finally, a piece of advice which was given to one of my students by a teacher in her Catholic Teaching Practice school: *Say a prayer on your way down the corridor to teach a difficult class.* The student had an excellent practice.

3

Already we begin to get the message that the successful teacher is the well-organised teacher. With younger children (say in the junior to middle age group of seven to twelve) actual disciplinary confrontations can almost be organised out of existence. What this means is simply that if a class is kept busy, so that there is always something waiting to be done, then the need to keep shouting for silence and to deliver diatribes about conduct and attitude will be reduced to a minimum. The best person to write about this kind of basic classroom organisation is a teacher who is currently doing the job, and yet who is still mentally in touch with his first months as a teacher.

Bob Jelley's memories of his first years of teaching are, not surprisingly, centred around one or two problem children who, to club myself with my own phrase, refused to be 'organised out of existence'. They imposed a tremendous strain upon his own self-confidence and also — this is quite common — caused him a great deal of worry about where his own responsibility ended and that of more senior members of staff began. Joe Newman has written about this self-same problem from the head's point of view. An early milestone in any teaching career comes when the teacher, already beset with doubts about himself, realises that the head is not infallible and may be hardly more equipped to deal with a particular problem child than the teacher himself. As a head working with talented colleagues, I feel this aspect of my relationship with them very keenly indeed.

One of my basic beliefs is that a teacher who has early disciplinary problems will in the end defeat them if he is basically a sane, well-balanced individual with a sense of humour and a liking for children — provided always that he is capable of a reasonable level of organisation. Many times have I offered this thought as comfort to a despairing young teacher and many times have I been proved right. Interestingly, the teacher himself may not perceive the improvement, failing to see that 'incidents' grow sparser; that classroom work improves and that the demeanour of the children grows happier and more willing. Sometimes, too, the young teacher fails to credit himself with the improvement, rationalising it in terms of 'a new class', 'a better room this year' or 'that rough lot eventually left'.

Let me say these things, then, to our young colleagues before they read Bob Jelley's piece.

(1) That most of us had trouble early on may be a cliché, but it is still true.

(2) Bob Jelley lay awake with individual children's faces swimming before him. So did we all. Did you think you were the only one who suffered in this way?

(3) Some teachers talk about a 'turning point'. They may actually claim to have hammered some child, after which 'everything was all right'. Let me say as strongly as I can that it is much more common for the improvement to be slow. Chinks of light appear rather than blinding visions. Is the second year better than the first? Is the third better than the second? This is the sort of time-scale we should be really thinking about.

(4) Remember what I said about the infallibility of headteachers. They can still help, of course. They have the power to move children from class to class, for example, or to bring in outside help. And because they have been in teaching a long time, they will have some useful advice to offer.

Running a Junior Classroom

BOB JELLEY

To start with, let me tell four short stories – two of them about student teachers and two of them about pupils. Later we can look at some of the links between the stories and draw some lessons from them. Other lessons and morals can, I suggest, be left implicit.

Arthur was a fellow student. Not given-over to lesson preparation he used to say, 'We've got our own rights, our own time'. In course work and exams he'd scrape through by last minute concentration and a calculated and sufficiently accurate insight into what our lecturers would like to hear.

Teaching practices were an irritation. Arthur trusted in a maxim which he called his Rommel principle – 'hold your best in reserve – until a lecturer comes; stick out most of it, do a bit of Maths, get them to read and perhaps do a project on castles or Tudors and Stuarts. When you get a lecturer in – reveal a carefully prepared lesson. Tutors aren't looking for trouble.' Anyway it all worked, Arthur passed through college and got a teaching post. I didn't hear from him for a while. When I did he was working in the Civil Service. He was quite objective about it all. His parents' thirst for their son to have a salaried, white-collar job was assuaged and 'you don't have to take work home'. When pressed he admitted that it had all finally got him down one day when he'd been pushed over-far by a child generally considered to be unruly. He had ended up on the floor in the story-corner wrestling. He said that suddenly it dawned on him that teaching was never going to be easy.

Nigel was another fellow student. His ticket through college was the 'Gilbert and Sullivan Society'. Membership of this society was said by the cynical to engender a cosy rapport between the few students who would join and a particularly musical Senior Common Room. So, though he did little work and was threatened with numerous reports to the Academic Board there seemed to be enough influential voices raised to constantly smooth things over.

Alas for Nigel the protective wing of the G. and S. Society didn't extend over the local schoolchildren. Throughout his first and second Teaching Practices there were stories told of Nigel's terror in the secondary moderns. One tale in particular had us all rolling in the aisles. Nigel's fellow student in one school said that on one occasion he'd gone looking for Nigel who was late for the Teaching Practice coach. Nigel was discovered entombed at the centre of an ingeniously constructed, precariously balanced pyramid of chairs and tables. The last I heard of him he was working in a bank, where he is no doubt a leading figure in the operatic society.

The third of the four stories concerns a pupil called Peter, a member of a class of thirty-five eight-year-olds. Generally uncared for, so far behind on standard tests that he always failed to score, his story shows the symptoms of inadequate mother love at home and inadequate remedial help at school.

Long-term problems of learning, however, could hardly be touched because of immediate problems of behaviour.

The worst moments came when Peter exploded; desks were dragged and chairs toppled backwards. He had black, glassy-eyed moods. Communication was shut down as he stared at the floor through sleep-encrusted eyes.

Go to the head? He would advise rightly, patience, under-standing and preparation. 'I'll have a word with Peter,' he would say with a paternal wink. Peter became increasingly aware of his teacher's exasperation and responded to it and his lone chat with the head by shrinking back further from his class teacher.

The teacher viewed himself as a lion-tamer watching for a worsening of the mood and then retreating quickly. Several activities carefully arranged for Peter received some response but there were days when for unknown reasons there was a total lack of response from the child from nine to three-thirty, regardless of how well-prepared the day was. Then it would be back to the Big Top with a red coat and a whip.

When the teacher went home he found Peter surfacing

again and again in conversation until the slightest mention of his name caused a row, and when he was sleeping Peter regularly turned up in dreams throwing chairs or eating the class' sticklebacks.

The following year and the year after, Peter was taught by newcomers to the profession. The staff satirist used to say that there was an initiation at the school, a ritual called 'Peter'. The staff wondered if the head was aware of the size of the problem, and eventually he called a case conference involving the Educational Psychologist.

On the very day of the conference, Peter stood in the rain in the playground defying efforts to coax him indoors which ended in an undignified chase. Eventually Peter was excluded from school and placed at a special boarding school.

Then there was Craig. He was possibly more difficult to manage, let alone teach, than Peter. He fought his way around the playgrounds throughout his first three years at middle school. He had little interest in anything except Go-Kart racing and his teachers tried to construct Maths and English and Reading schemes around the theme of Go-Kart racing. Given classes of thirty-eight, Craig's teachers made sorties against his apathy but they were fighting on too many other fronts and invariably Craig would be allowed to sit staring blankly. His apathy was one thing but the other thirty-seven children in his class obviously deserved a proportion of their teacher's time. If the class doesn't get that attention then other problems will arise springing from children being under occupied, work not marked and particular academic difficulties not explained. The dutiful concern of the head and visiting experts did not lead to any extra assistance being given to Craig's teacher.

Craig said little but consistently smiled throughout the many heart to heart interviews which he had with a line of visitors. He came from a home which dressed him well and appeared to love him fondly. He may have been over lavished with material possessions – spoilt in the way that, as is often alleged, only-children are spoilt, but these factors hardly explained the extremity of his disinclination to show interest in any aspect of school apart from playground fighting. As Craig entered the fourth year the heat of his tempers raged fiercer and his tempers became more frequent.

Craig was in a fourth year class with thirty-eight other children housed in a temporary hut. His teacher – very competent and caring – became determined to make the head at least realise the extent of the problems created by having Craig in the class.

How could the head taste how bitter it was to teach Craig without teaching him for a year himself? The best that could be done from the class teacher's view was to send Craig along to the head as often as his temper necessitated it. At first he'd return sober, stilled for what must have been jewelled moments of peace, but gradually the pace picked up.

Trauma followed trauma. Dinner ladies were abused indiscriminately. Children were regularly assaulted. Parents of the assailant visited regularly. Parents of the assaulted were pacified. The head was clearly expending time and energy on the problem but Craig was still present in the classroom, a figure of doom in the corner of the room. So, as with the story of Peter, the molecular structure of the staffroom became agitated.

The head put in mental and physical work, but from the vantage point of the staffroom, a suspicion inevitably arises at such times that heads will put off invoking the exclusion procedure. Perhaps heads are at times less worried about the problems of the class teacher than they are about their own role in an exclusion case.

Other teachers were consulted, and prevailed upon to bring talents to bear. While these negotiations were going on Craig was contributing little to his own sales campaign. Eventually a finale was enacted involving a bitter fight between Craig and another pupil and he was excluded because no teacher would accept him back in class.

It seems to me that the two tottering students and the two problem pupils together highlight one very important point. This is that whereas in theory there may be no pupil who cannot be taught and no class which cannot be won over, the reality is that some problems *are* insurmountable. Stories like the two about Peter and Craig might well be told to probationary teachers in orders to prepare them for the extreme possibilities which lie ahead.

On the other hand naming the foe, identifying the problem,

is no complete solution. It's often said that knowing a problem exists means that you are half-way towards solving the problem itself. A difficult maxim this and a dangerous one to adopt with respect to the kind of discipline problems that I have described. For once the problem has been spotlighted, the nightmare named, then immediate action is also necessary if only to make the class teacher realise that his perseverance is known, respected and is being reinforced. Consider the story about Peter. The teacher was constantly being told about the boy's home life. Headteacher, parents and social service visitors all admitted that Peter was an enigma. Indeed his parents confessed that they were unable to 'get on' with their son. Nevertheless the problem was not inactivated. Each day Peter was there in the class ready to do battle. The class teacher was unable to turn his understanding of the problem into an easing of it.

Bluntly, the only hope which most teachers have of coping with the extreme cases is if they receive some positive help. This means, for example:

(1) Extra help for the class teacher – the provision of an extra teacher who can work in the classroom and allow the class teacher to give at least some of his attention to the rest of the class.

(2) Withdrawal of children with difficulties. Again, this implies the provision of extra staff.

(3) Help in the preparation of an individual scheme of work for the difficult child.

The point is that having a meeting does not, of itself, *solve* anything, and the teacher who starts out attending them willingly and hopefully may in the end become disgruntled and unwilling if nothing positive happens afterwards. Attendance at meetings can become an added burden.

Fortunately, not all the problems are insurmountable; not every class contains its Craig or Peter. When we consider the task of teaching a class free of the kind of single dominating difficulty described, then discipline may be seen as taking a back seat. It is a factor to be taken into consideration along with others.

The consistent relationship is that between Organisation and Discipline. The story of the two students illustrates this –

they were not organised, and they had discipline problems. Even in the case of Peter and Craig, the point was that they disrupted the organisation of their classes.

To examine this relationship and to elaborate on what I mean by Organisation, it would be useful to look at one or two situations which might occur in most schools.

Take, first of all, the prospect of restarting after the lunch hour. As afternoon approaches, I consider my own approach towards it. On one occasion I walk energetically through the school in plenty of time, returning 250 'helloes' and refusing countless boiled sweets. Then as the bell goes, I await the arrival of the children. Some come in quietly, others always noisily. How do I react to this? If in a resilient mood I absorb the noise into a joke; if brittle, I put down the songster and eyes dart across with the unspoken message about 'Sir's mood'.

Or perhaps I come down the corridor late, after classes have entered. Tables are askew, the floor is littered with chess-pieces, noise is high and movement is considerable. Where do I start?

What are the lessons from what has been said so far? To begin with, I reiterate the old adage about the need for being consistent. What deserves a reprimand one day should deserve it the next. Fortunately, children are resilient, and do recognise the fallibility of their teacher. Nevertheless, we ought to try for consistency of approach between one day and another, one class and another, one pupil and another.

The answer to the second problem – that of arriving late to find near-chaos – is that, of course, it should not arise in the first place. Ideally, the teacher is always in his room before the children. In the imperfect world, he may be delayed. Even so, the problems are considerably lessened if children are always dismissed knowing what work they have to return to. At the very least, the following could apply:

(1) Every child should know where he is in the Maths scheme, and where he should have reached by say, the end of the week; he has a target which spare time helps him to reach.

(2) Some children might be in the process of writing a long story, with a definite date in mind for its completion; chapter 1 by Thursday, chapter 2 by Tuesday.

(3) There could be a current project work-card in every child's desk.

It is relatively easy to think of tasks like this. They can be reinforced by being written up on a chart, or simply on the blackboard, or in the form of individual work-cards. As important as providing the work, is the need to train the class to the habit of 'getting on' when the need arises. This in turn implies recognising and rewarding those children who do 'get on'. A teacher of some experience, where I teach now often leaves his class purposely and judges, from nearby, how they can get on without him.

An unavoidable implication of long-term work targets for children is that the teacher should have long-term targets of his own clearly thought out. Given the absence of preparation time, most primary teachers feel that they have to give up more and more of their own time to prepare. Any planning I do repays the original investment of time one hundred per cent. In particular, planning stops moments of panic and much self questioning: 'Why am I doing this? I haven't done any practical weighing work. We still haven't covered speech marks.' The more careful the planning, the less the need for scrambled 'catching up' later on.

It follows for me that if planning and preparation are so important, then headteachers and those above them will need to arrange matters so that teachers do not think of preparation as being synonymous with unpaid overtime. There is a clear necessity for regular, preferably daily, preparation periods for all teachers.

Also in question here is the degree to which a teacher's work should be prescribed by school schemes or syllabuses. Too much prescription risks losing the opportunity for spontaneity and for seizing the unexpected happening. There is in English education a 'king in his own classroom' theory which sees lack of structure and uniformity as one of the glories of the system, akin to the noble principle of intellectual freedom. It is possible to have some sympathy with this view, at the same time feeling that an eight-year-old non-reader needs intellectual freedom less than he needs an organised reading scheme and a structured remedial back-up.

Here is another example of what happens when you fail to

organise. After lunch one day I returned to the class having been delayed by a discussion of Coventry City's new centre half. The fourth year area was united in disruption; five tig games were in progress, there were heated realignments of romantic attachments and Pascoe-like desk jumping. As the deputy head went by me she pointedly ignored me and that silent criticism amplified the noise which my class was making even further. My temperature and pulse responded and a chain of events was set in motion.

I yelled at David who had let his new sharp Maths pencil drop to the floor. The class cowered sensing my mood. Five minutes later David was experiencing an asthmatic attack. I carried him out and spent ten minutes in the staffroom reassuring him and getting his breathing deep and his forehead cool. Meanwhile in the classroom Gary had reacted to the drama in macabre style chanting 'David is dying' accompanied by a rhythmical handclap. Steven assumed the mantle of outraged moralist and clobbered Gary who decided to flee home. Having calmed David I returned to the class (thinking that the situation would have eased) to find escalating drama.

That afternoon won the award as being the worst of 1978. It was only after a few days, when I'd stopped shaking, that I managed to conduct a reasoned appraisal of the events. What had gone wrong? For a start let me suggest the following:

(1) All this happened in the pre-Christmas rush which affects every teacher. On such occasions more organisation is needed rather than less. With disruption to the timetable caused by rehearsals and film shows, children need to be told firmly and clearly in advance what is going to happen next. If not, the idea that 'anything goes' will quickly become established.

(2) The teacher's own feeling of frustration and disorganisation should not be communicated to the children as bad temper and recrimination. If it is, they will be hurt and may well hit back if the opportunity arises.

There are many other factors, more intangible than those so far described, which influence the atmosphere in a classroom and contribute positively or negatively towards order, discipline and the general climate of the classroom. The personality of the teacher is important, of course – as in this example:

This week I have been introducing the concept of pi to a class of fourth year middle school twelve-year-olds. It's been a trip down Memory Lane looking at the initial – and in some cases lasting – looks of confusion, and remembering my own introduction to the same subject.

I met pi in my first years of secondary school. I had performed well in the four rules and mental arithmetic tests at my junior school but this new Maths (this algebra and this pi) was beyond my understanding. The way I later learnt to deal with it was as a jigsaw puzzle, then it all fell into place. I'd get the hang of things just as the rest of the set were on to algebra or equations or the use of logarithmic books – how we hated the compiler of those books and cut insults to him deep into our desks.

Though I myself could just about manage the Maths, one or two of us carried those lasting, confused looks. Most unfortunate of all was Jeff Brush. He turned probability theory upside down. The torment of Jeff Brush would come with every Maths lesson. The Maths teacher would shuffle into the room, crash a pile of books dramatically down onto the table and fire questions around as a sort of warm-up. Most of these would be delivered from a standing position. The sign that the preamble was over was the master's slow walk towards Jeff Brush's desk:

'Circumference of a circle Brush?'

'Area of a circle Brush?'

Every lesson – daily ritual – the questions were asked. Remarkably, astonishingly despite a fifty per cent chance of success Jeff Brush would give the wrong answer. Then he would be beaten around the head, his tormentor accompanying each blow with a syllable of the correct formula:

Bang 'Two' *bang* 'pi' *bang* 'R' *bang* 'Brush' *bang*.

It was then a most welcome part of the day for the rest of us. A ritual, nightmarish to reflect on but an entertaining change at the time.

Despite all the intimidation and fear, this teacher would according to some criteria be judged as having 'good discipline'. His class was always quiet, for example, and I suspect that despite all modern ideas about talk and movement, keeping the class quiet continues to be a way by which teachers expect to get the approval of their colleagues.

The message in this, I suggest, is that any one of us may be tempted to plump for the easy choice: simply browbeat our classes into the severely silent units of immobility which can still be found here and there. The disadvantages of this approach hardly need reiteration, but for the sake of clarity I include some of them as:

(1) In a silent classroom the child who does not understand cannot make his problem known.

(2) If the children fear the teacher they may learn how to tell him what he wants to hear, but there will be no learning in the fuller sense.

(3) The teacher's judgments of his children will be based on a very narrow band of responses. Less obvious qualities will never surface.

The alternative to this, I suggest, is a classroom where each child can ask the questions he needs to ask and can do the work he needs to do. That this implies good organisation hardly needs repeating. Consider what is needed.

(1) Each child must be able to question the teacher. This means that other children must have work to do while this is going on. One result of failing in this bit of organisation is the long queue at the teacher's desk, with the child at the back being unattended for, perhaps, half the lesson.

(2) Each child must know what to do when the immediate task is completed.

(3) The materials for each task must be available.

(4) Some system for marking the work must be devised, and this must be manageable – staying up to one a.m. marking every night is as much an indictment of standard of organisation as is doing no marking at all. In turn, this implies the development and running of various self-marking systems and the balanced use of work which needs detailed marking against that which needs little or none. Some kinds of classroom work – exercises or blackboard tasks – need little attention while being done but set a tremendous marking burden afterwards. It is too easy to slip into setting these for various short-term reasons while overlooking the need to spend hours marking them. The danger then arises of setting them and not marking them. Children rapidly become wise to this, and the

standard of work and behaviour suffers accordingly.

But criticism of other teachers is easy to make. It's simple to draw little caricatures and ridicule people and their ideas. It is more difficult to formulate your own ideas, organise them into a structure and then apply that structure and those ideas daily throughout a long career. My own objectives and aspirations with regard to the job are very slow in crystallising. There is the emergence of the strong belief that organisation and discipline go together.

My own record at organising is mixed. I seem to spend hours of my own time at school or doing schoolwork at home. Yet I would never say that I am well-organised. My various bosses – LEA, Dept of Ed, headteacher – barely repay me for my 'overtime'. I am entitled to no statutory free periods. Despite all the reports which talk of offering in-service training for this course or that subject, most of the time it seems to be expected that I will give up my own time to attend. Asking for smaller classes seems to be synonymous in some quarters with admitting membership of the Baader Meinhof Gang.

On the one hand children are being raised in a democracy, so called, on the other hand they may be dragooned in learning. On the one hand children should be encouraged to think for themselves and have an inner-discipline and on the other hand they may be expected to think as part of a class-unit with little effective opportunity to think at a tangent to the class and teacher.

Individual learning schemes and structures with all the extra teachers and preparation periods that they would have to be based on can be the key to organisational improvements in the classrooms. And given improvements in the inducements to teachers to organise, there lies the most evident possibility of the encouragement of self-discipline in the children we teach.

4

Sticks, Carrots and Peruvian Hot Water

GERALD HAIGH

A concept which has always interested me is that of 'cultural
dissonance'. The best example I have heard of concerns some
medical aides from the United States who visited a Peruvian
mountain village. Among other things, they tried to persuade
the local people to boil their water before drinking it. It
seemed an obvious, commonsense sort of thing to do. In fact
their effort to introduce this apparently simple precaution
failed totally, because there was in the village a traditional
belief, much stronger than commonsense, that water which
was, or had been, warm was associated with weakness and
would weaken the person taking it. Every teacher, it seems to
me, should think on this story. How often do we point out to
our pupils all manner of apparently obvious and sensible
things only to find that they are received as if we had flown
directly from Venus with them?

Three little scenes from school life, before we go any further.
In the first, a boy swears at another in the corridor and a
passing teacher reacts with shock and anger. In the second a
group of girls are admonished by a senior mistress for wearing
nail varnish. In the third a teacher screws up his face with
disgust and orders a pupil to get rid of his chewing gum.

Each of these is highly typical. You could see any one of
them being enacted on any single day in just about any state
school. They are prime examples, it seems to me, of cultural
dissonance. To the boy who swore, after all, or to the girls with
coloured nails and the pupil chewing gum, their behaviour
was natural and normal. To the teachers who disciplined
them, the same behaviour seemed so obviously distasteful that
correction had no need of explanation. What happens most of
the time is that the 'comprehension gap' is accepted and

absorbed, just as a village in the end learns to live with a motorway through the middle. What this means is that the teachers see pupils as exasperating beings who have to be told obvious things, and who yet refuse to cooperate of their own free will. The pupils, for their part, begin to see school as a funny sort of place filled with unpredictable and arbitrary hazards, a bit like the Noah's Ark in the South Shore amusement park at Blackpool, where one minute a solid looking staircase shakes and the next a jet of cold air blows up your leg.

To some extent, of course, the dissonance is based on social class. The majority of state school pupils are of working-class origin – a simple statistical fact this; not only is the working-class band of the population the broadest one, but those pupils who are bought out of the state system are overwhelmingly *not* working-class. Schools, on the other hand, are middle-class institutions. I do not think this is a matter for serious dispute; it is not just that teaching is a middle-class job but that the traditions and values of formal education are inextricably bound up with the traditions and values of what we have come to regard as the middle-class way of life. Belief in future reward for present toil is just one aspect of this.

This latter concept is important enough to examine further. When you think about it, a school is a place which depends heavily on the notion of deferred gratification – the idea that if you do the right thing now, then at some time in the future there will be rewards. The end of term report; the house point trophy; the end of year exam are all dangled, carrot-fashion, as motivators. The ultimate deferred reward, though, is that of success in public examinations together with the assumption that this leads on to a good job. 'Work hard and you'll get a good job' is the simple way of putting it, and it has been exactly thus expressed by many generations of secondary school teachers. Any long-serving head or senior teacher will have lost count of the number of failing, unwilling pupils he has carpeted and tried to reform by means of talk about 'future prospects' and predictions of the regret and remorse which will, it is said, suddenly appear at the age of seventeen.

The assumption here is that of the 'career' – the idea that total fulfilment in life is attained by mounting a ladder of vocational success. Seen in this way, a job which is not at the foot of a clearly defined ladder is a 'dead-end job' and, it follows, one to be avoided by all right thinking youngsters. Thus does it become axiomatic that a badly paid apprenticeship is a 'better prospect' than a well paid 'dead-end' job – again, you see, the notion of deferred gratification.

Criticism of this way of looking at life has, of course, to be very carefully done – especially by someone who has passed a lot of exams, gained a lot of promotions and become a headmaster. At the same time, it seems quite obvious to me that a very large number of people do work in dead-end jobs and do not see life in terms of 'a career' at all. To suggest that all of these people are unhappy and unfulfilled would be to insult them and to place much too narrow an interpretation on what life is all about. I do not want to get into too patronising a position about this. All I want to say, quite simply, is that if a fourteen-year-old boy lives among adults who do semi-skilled 'non-career' jobs, and yet who have happy homes and full social lives, then we cannot take it for granted that we will easily motivate him by suggesting that there is something better. The same holds, I might say, even if the adults concerned support our view, as they often do.

In recent years the position has been complicated by the increase in unemployment, so that in many parts of the country it is simply not true that hard work and good reports will ensure a good job. If, in an outburst of total honesty, we have to say to our pupils 'no matter how hard you work it really will not make much difference,' then where does that leave us?

In any case, for many pupils the inappropriateness of deferred gratification as a motivator is not dependent upon cultural or social considerations at all. When you think about it, to tell any child that the reward for his good work will come at some distant time in the future, is to impose quite a strain upon his way of working and thinking. Most children simply do not operate like that, and distant reward becomes less effective the younger or less intelligent the child is. It works the other way, too, so that there is little to be gained from telling an eight-year-old that if he misbehaves now, he will miss his games lesson in three days time. For many children this is about as sensible as threatening to ban him from an expedition to the moon in the year 2002. The cultural point is, though, that the child who is most likely to be impressed at all by this not-too-efficient method of motivation is the one who has been brought up in an environment where deferred gratification and the concept of the career are part of the way of life – and this means the child from a middle-class home.

In practical terms, the way that all this is worked out in school is that there are many children for whom the basic motivator of 'work hard for future reward' cuts little or no ice. The astonishing thing is that it continues to be such a basic part of school life.

Most schools, then, operate by rewards and punishments – by positive and negative reinforcements. The rewards, though, as we have seen, are mainly long-deferred, and as such more acceptable to middle-class pupils. What short-term rewards are there, of a kind which might be generally effective? Many teachers, I suggest, might be uneasy at this question, because it is often true to say that while a school has a system for punishments, it does not have a system of rewards. Many would say that the best reward is the approval of a respected teacher. This may be so, but it is equally true that the withdrawal of this approval might be the best sort of punishment, and yet many schools feel the need to supplement this with a punishment system. Why, then, do they not feel the need to reinforce the teacher's approval with a system of tangible rewards?

Part of the answer to this is, I am convinced, also cultural in nature, and has to do with puritanical notions about the nature of work. The idea that work is good of itself and requires no reward is deeply ingrained in us. We are constantly told that if councillors or magistrates or teachers or nurses were properly paid for what they were doing, then we would get all kinds of nasty people muscling in to do the jobs for the money. The way that this works at school level is that many teachers are very uneasy about rewarding children for doing what they ought to have been doing in the first place. A reward for exceptional work or behaviour above and beyond, as it were, the call of duty is one thing. A reward for doing what some children do without reward is quite another. This, in fact, is what makes many people uneasy about giving special attention to disturbed or disrupting children. One child may work all day without chiding or praise. Another, because his conduct is usually intolerable, may be praised or actually rewarded for sitting still for ten minutes. Many of our colleagues find this very difficult to take.

Institutionalised rewards in school – other than those used by visiting educational psychologists, or under their supervision – are very sparse. There is, of course, the teacher's word of praise, or comment written on a piece of work, and this is not to be despised. You have to look hard, though, to find the obverse of the not uncommon punishment system which uses, in a planned way, sending to the Head of Department or House Head, sending to the Head, impositions, detention and beating, the whole explicitly arranged on a hierarchical scale so that the child who commits a particular crime knows roughly what punishment to expect.

Eton used to have a system called 'sending up for good' – perhaps they still do. A pupil went to the Head with a piece of work neatly written on school notepaper. The point is that this was a *system* rather than a casual occasional happening. In my experience, systems like this are very rare.

Young children are often given 'stars' or special marks. Sometimes these are then totted up and entered on a chart on the wall. Teachers are beset by doubts, though, even about such simple devices as this. In particular they worry about the way that a clever child may have a row of stars marching across the chart while another hardly gets off the start line. In practice, they compensate for this by giving stars for good effort rather than for naked brilliance (again, the puritan ethic creeping in). Rarely, in my experience, are stars used as rewards for good *behaviour*.

In secondary schools, individual awards of reward points or marks are invariably linked to a house system. The house system itself, of course, is based on very middle-class assumptions about team work and healthy competition. The idea is that a pupil doing something worth rewarding gets a point for his team. Supporting his house in this way is supposed to give him satisfaction, and probably does, although children do tend to see house points as individual rather than team rewards.

Again, house points are not often given simply for accept-able behaviour. Interestingly, though, there are teachers who will *subtract* house points for *bad* behaviour. This is usually a singularly ineffective punishment, mainly because of the surely rather obvious fact that a child who behaves badly is probably not one to be over-imbued with the team-ethic which is supposed to underpin the house point system. This some-times leads to the absurd spectacle of a weak teacher removing house points wholesale at a faster rate than they are being won by the hard-working pupils. It is for this reason that many schools have banned the use of house point subtraction as a punishment.

It becomes clear, I think, that while many, perhaps most, schools will punish bad behaviour and to some extent reward good work, few schools will *reward good behaviour*. Admittedly there are intrinsic rewards – teacher attitude and approval being the main one – but overt hierarchical reward systems parallel to the overt hierarchical punishment systems do not on the whole exist.

This is a serious deficiency, given the premiss from which I started – that the working-class pupil is not at all likely to be motivated into a positive attitude by the long-term reward mechanism which society and school already provide.

If we began to consider the kind of contingent rewards which *could* be provided then we would, I suspect, begin to run into ethical difficulties again. The same puritanism which has reared its head before would suggest that while it may be all right to choose punishments which children dislike, it would be much less acceptable to choose rewards which the children wanted. Detention, for instance, is inconvenient to the teachers who run it, to parents and to the caretaking staff, but schools persevere with it because it is supposed to be irksome to the children who are being punished. If we were to examine children's wishes about suitable rewards for good behaviour we might find that house points and certificates had to con-tend with free sweets, extra playtime, going home early and legalised absence from unpopular lessons. Not many teachers, I guess, would want to get too deeply enmeshed in the rights and wrongs of many of these. Many rewards would, though, be clearly acceptable to most people on both sides of the transaction – badges, certificates, labelled ball pens and pencils come to mind for example.

The problems are still great, however. The cry of 'bribery' is bound to go up in any discussion of rewarding acceptable behaviour. And if rewards are given for *improved* behaviour rather than simply for the attainment of a generally enforced standard, then clearly some pupils will be rewarded and others not, even though their behaviour may be, objectively, equally good. There will also be many teachers who are worried about the sheer materialism of it all, and the implicit acceptance of what seems to be a selfishly competitive ethic. At the root of these doubts lies the classic dilemma surrounding the behaviourist philosophy – that while you may, quite easily, obtain the behavioural changes you want, what have you done to secure the *attitudes* which you want? I can best illustrate this, I suppose, by offering the following imaginary conversation:

Teacher A   I propose to modify the behaviour of my class by rewarding the behaviours I want. I shall have a system of points, certificates and small gifts.

Teacher B   This may get them quiet and attentive to their work, but will it make them warm and considerate to each other?

Teacher A   Behavioural modification will do whatever you want it to. I want them to be considerate and cooperative, therefore I shall reward considerate and cooperative behaviour.

Teacher B   Then you will end up with *behaviour* which is warm and considerate, but will you have *children* who are warm and considerate?

There is, I suggest, literally no answer to that, because by definition if we are working on behaviour then we are not concerned with inner motives. Let it be said, though, that many teachers, faced with unruly children, would settle for a class which behaved acceptably, whatever was going on in their hearts and minds.

It is also true that if this argument can be used against reward systems, it can also be used against punishments. In what sense can you *beat* children into being kind and considerate to each other?

Now before I get too deeply enmeshed in the philosophical implications of all this, it is probably time to lay down one or two working principles arising out of what has been said already and looking forward to the discussion still to come. These are:

(1) If we are going to have carefully thought out punishment systems in school, then it makes as much sense to have carefully thought out reward systems. My experience is that rewards work at least as well as punishments and are much more pleasant!

(2) There will be ethical problems over rewards, but if a sense of balance and proportion is kept, then these should not be greater than the ethical and moral problems caused by punishment systems.

(3) Although I have said various things about 'behaviour' and 'behavioural modification', I have not really been discussing this in a psychologically scientific way. I leave this to Dr Ron Fawcett who provides a paper on the subject later in the book.

(4) In so far as both rewards and punishments are devices for manipulating behaviour, then we must see them as only a small part of the educative process, for education is about much more inward things. Nevertheless there are times when manipulation is necessary.

(5) We must bear in mind that the traditional ultimate reward of diligence – success in life – is not only irrelevant to many pupils, but is probably not even a true statement of the case any more. We must provide more contingent and relevant rewards for our pupils. If we do not, then we seem to be dependent only upon punishment. Is this what we want?

Before considering what all this might mean to the classroom teacher, there is another aspect of cultural dissonance which affects us. This is brought about by the simple fact that as teachers we are adults dealing with children. If anyone thinks this is too simplistic a notion to bear discussion, let him consider the number of times that teachers have been heard to accuse children of being – of all things – *childish*.

It is all too common to forget that children are not adults

and, into the bargain, forget that we were ever children ourselves. Bus conductors, swimming pool attendants, park keep-
ers, as well as some teachers, are too commonly afflicted by
what ought to be called the W. C. Fields Syndrome. At its
worst the WCF Syndrome is marked by a tendency to be
nervously aggressive towards children long before they have
ever done anything wrong – like the bus driver who threatens
his young charges with all sorts of retribution as soon as they
get on board, and is then surprised when they needle him in a
thousand hardly detectable ways throughout the journey. The
fact of the matter is that if you put fifty young people who
know each other on a bus together they will inevitably be
noisy and boisterous. Whether or not you regard this as inso-
lence and ill manners depends upon how strongly afflicted you
are by the WCFS. (It is worth considering, incidentally, what
is likely to mark out the behaviour of, say, fifty salesmen on a
bus journey together. Better still, ask some bus drivers which
group of passengers they would rather take.)

Sometimes, to extend the metaphor a bit, the W. C. Fields
Syndrome deepens and broadens into what I will call the
'Thin End of the Wedge' or 'Yellow Peril' syndrome. This is
the state of affairs in which people in charge of children – be
they teachers, scout leaders or whatever – see their charges as
potential insurrectionists. Within this ideology, every pec-
cadillo has to be 'cracked down on' so that it can be clearly
seen who is in charge and who is underneath. To allow something apparently trivial to pass may be 'The Thin End of the
Wedge'. As you talk to teachers you become aware that this
Thin End may take many forms. It may consist of pierced ears
with earrings, or striped socks, or coming into school without
lining up, or failing to say 'Sir', or leaning against a wall or
speaking at the wrong moment.

Now while discipline manifestly has to be kept, and while a
small action may have important implications, I think we
would do well to remind ourselves that too much defensive-
ness, too much standing upon dignity, too much outrage over
trivialities is, in the end, ridiculous and in itself undignified. It
is no coincidence that humorous writers have homed uner-
ringly in on the image of the schoolmaster incoherent with
rage over the mildest of offences, and the formula beginning

'It has come to my notice that certain boys . . .' is a useful standby for anything from Monty Python to a great satirical novel.

We would all do well to remember, I think, that a child is a person who would just as soon run as walk; who would just as soon shout as whisper; who would just as soon interrupt as wait his turn; who would just as soon lash out as indulge in sophistry. Of course, it is part of the growing-up process that he should learn how to moderate some of these tendencies, but we must remember that he will not learn all at once and that growing maturity must be matched by growing trust. In school terms this may mean that if one child over-reaches himself and smashes a light fitting with a basketball during break, it may not be either necessary or appropriate for the whole school to be subjected to a self-righteous and outraged lecture about how to behave.

We must continually remind ourselves, too, that while some childish characteristics might be unattractive others are very attractive indeed, and we would do well not to stamp them all out indiscriminately. We could consider, too, the fact that as childish characteristics recede, the adult characteristics which replace them may not, to say the least, be always desirable. The teacher who says to a child, 'It's time you grew up' may be wishing upon him a set of very mixed blessings.

When the pupils involved are teenagers – secondary school students in particular – the 'generation gap' has its own peculiarities. The gulf between the working-class, urban sixteen-year-old and his forty-year-old grammar school and university educated form master may be a very wide one indeed.

It is time to turn to the classroom implications of some of the things which I have said. The best way to do this is to set out a list of 'working principles for the young teacher'. He or she does not have to swallow them whole, but at the very least they offer a jumping off point for discussion.

(1) Do not constantly lecture pupils about the dismal future which awaits them if they do not behave well and work hard. Such a speech will sound to most classes like a well-worn gramophone record – part of the irrelevant and half-heard teacher-produced Muzak which fills the ears of many pupils

while they are in school. There are children who may be impressed by such talk, but they are not likely to be the ones who
are giving much trouble. By and large, the children or young
people who give *real* trouble in school are highly unlikely to be
affected by any long-distance motivators at all — be they
threats of hell or promises of heaven.

(2) It follows logically that rewards and punishments must
be immediate in effect — or as nearly so as possible.

(3) Again, logically, it follows that if you have thought out
and considered methods of punishment, then you must
equally think out and consider methods of reward. This is very
important. Many teachers, upon encountering their first disciplinary problems, think entirely in terms of punishment. Joe
Newman, in his paper in this book, tells how often the new
teacher asks what the disciplinary system is. Whatever
rewards are used will depend on the age of the children and
the type of school. There are general principles, however, the
first of which is that it makes obvious sense to use whatever
methods are already in existence. This will usually mean stars
or house points, depending on age. Use them systematically
and predictably, and do not be inhibited by false puritanism
into being too mean with them.

(4) Bolster up the school's reward system by introducing
methods of your own. You could, for instance, run off some
simple certificates or make some badges. One of my colleagues
has a toy called 'Harry the Hippo' which stands proudly each
day on the table occupied by the children who worked best the
previous day, the award being decided by the very liberal use
of points. It is worth bearing in mind, by the way, that if the
only points used are house points, then teachers may be inhibited from using them liberally because of the implications for
trophies and important house 'positions' beyond the classroom. What I like about Harry the Hippo and other kindred
devices is that they accept that children are children and not
gloomy adults who believe that all trophies should be cup-
shaped. They also accept that the average child sees a funny
toy as a more realistic reward than the promise of being a
solicitor's articled clerk in five years' time.

(5) Do not make too many middle-class judgments about
things like 'manners'. Of course good manners are important,

but the people who traditionally have shaped them have always believed that they spring from consideration to others, and should never be used as a weapon for scorn or outrage. Manners are best taught by projection and example. The teacher who viciously berates children for their lack of manners is being ill-mannered himself.

In the same way, a teacher has to know when to splutter with rage and when not. I recall vividly how when I was at school we carried out what would now rank as a major piece of experimental psychology. We baited the top of the classroom door with a falling book for every teacher we had that day, and noted their reactions. Already I think you can guess at the result. The ones who railed and hurled the book about were the weaklings and broken reeds. The most awe-inspiring disciplinarian walked through the book as if it were not there, and acknowledged the incident in no overt way at all except that – and we all knew – he screwed up the already hypersonic tension of his hold over us by just one tiny fraction of a degree for the whole of the lesson.

Work very hard, therefore, at judging how and when to react, and indulge in careful self-searching after the event. Remember that one hallmark of the uncertain teacher is that he will let things slip for a long while and will then suddenly impose draconian punishments for insignificant acts of naughtiness. All new teachers are likely to do this. What is important is that they realise they have done it, and use the experience to build a more mature set of reactions.

(6) Do not take good and co-operative conduct for granted – use your reward system to encourage it. The basic – and perhaps in the end the most important – reward is a word of approval from you. Let me give an everyday example.

Almost every teacher will, several times a day, enter a classroom full of children who are waiting for him. Ideally, he would like these children to be working, or at least not actually racing around the room, when he arrives. Many teachers would deal with this by coming into the room and bawling for silence, or perhaps waiting menacingly with folded arms. This would be followed by a five-minute lecture on how to behave when waiting for sir. If things have been particularly bad, then individuals might be punished. Then the next day, or even later the same day, the whole performance will be repeated.

If you are a young teacher, the chances are that this little scenario is a common, almost unconsidered, part of your existence.

Why not try this instead? As you approach the room, or as you are entering it, before you have even noticed individual children, you say clearly and warmly,

'There are some children here doing the right thing; that's what I like to see.'

At this, one or two children will begin to read books or write. Instantly you point to them, and still without shouting you say,

'There's somebody reading, good! There's somebody else. Well done!'

At this, several other children, having either heard or seen the exchanges, will also take up books and pens.

'There's somebody else!' you say, 'Excellent!'

Given a reasonable basic level of order, the odds are that you will have to tell nobody off; that the class will be reduced to silent attention in considerably less time than it takes to read this description – and certainly less time than it would take to bully them into silence; and that the atmosphere for the start of the lesson will be almost tangibly warmer than it would otherwise have been. All this seems obvious to me. So much so that it is perhaps necessary to remind any non-teaching readers that this kind of positive, rewarding, approach to children is far less common than it should be.

This approach could be institutionalised by means of points for the 'best' group of children, converted later into certificates or into something to stand on the table. The feelings of my readers towards doing this will probably vary, but there will undoubtedly be some who are desperately racking their brains for a way of getting out of a vicious circle of nagging and recrimination. This that I have described, or a personal modification of it, is a pointer to the way out.

(7) Never ever forget that children are not adults. They do not shout or run or push past out of vindictiveness or self-preservation. They do it simply because they have not grown up yet.

(8) Do not forget, either, that adolescents are often much more like children than either they or you might think. Sophistication is a very thin veneer, and is often gratefully cast off if only for a short time.

(9) Do not try to cross the generation gap by being a teenager yourself. Nothing is more pathetic or more transparent. You have to perceive the gap, understand it and see across it. You do not have to try to leap it.

(10) Examine the punishment system very carefully. In English schools, the following are likely to be found as institutionalised punishments:

(a) Detention. This means keeping children in after school. Usually, teachers take it in turn to supervise detention. Typically, a child misbehaves, teacher says, 'Detention, Marjorie!' and then gives Marjorie a piece of paper or form detailing the offence and providing a space for parental signature. The detention is also entered in a book which is brought to the detention session by the teacher in charge. As a teacher supervising detention, I was always amused by the number of children who waited outside the room for their friends, or who actually came up and asked if they could sit in and wait.

(b) Impositions. This is the public school term for extra work. Traditionally it involved the writing of interminable and deliberately dreary 'lines' – 'I must not talk in class' being one of the simpler ones. Fifty, a hundred or two hundred lines could be given, with occasional forays into the stratospheric realms of five hundred or even a thousand.

(c) Beating. Still very much alive in British schools, especially for pupils between eleven and sixteen. Few inexperienced teachers beat children these days, though, because the actual administration is usually – though not always – in the hands of senior teachers. There are local authority rules about beating. These are sometimes broken, but should never be transgressed by a young teacher who wants to keep the support of his head or his employers. Sometimes it is said that beating is dying out. Certainly it happens much less than it used to, but I feel certain that its ultimate demise will only be brought about by legislation against the wishes of at least a substantial minority of teachers.

Every teacher, I think, has to come to terms with the fact that punishment, as a concept and a practice, has little to do with education. The thinking teacher punishes (with reluctance) because, firstly, he has a lot of pupils to look after and to punish one may free him to consider the others; secondly because he does not have the time to do anything more constructive; and thirdly because he feels inadequate, given the circumstances within which he works, to cope with an immediate problem in any other way.

For many, I suppose, I am not nearly radical enough. Having said that cultural dissonance exists and that it is at least in part due to the middle-class nature of schools, it will be said that I ought to go on and propose radical changes. I am not sure how far you can go with that and still end up with something which is recognisably a school. This is why I have always held that de-schooling was a more honest philosophy than one which tries to create, say, schools with working-class characteristics. Many middle-class attributes – and aristocratic attributes for that matter – are desirable. What we have to do is to remember that they may not be accepted totally and automatically by the pupils. In the end, after all, the Peruvians *would* have been better off boiling their water. It simply needed a bit more time, a bit more understanding and a bit more self-analysis by the teachers to get them to do it.

5

In the last paper, I discussed the, for me, fascinating concept of 'cultural dissonance'. The idea that cultural groups and sub-groups can rub and prickle upon one another in a way that might be potentially destructive, but can also be stimulating and creative, is something which we all have to learn if we are to cope with today's society. One obvious aspect of this is the dimension brought about by the presence of minority ethnic groups. The impact of these on our society has been enormous, and our nation is at this very moment going through the agonising pangs caused by its need to re-identify itself as a multi-cultural community. 'Perhaps it always was one' is one facile possibility here, but even so it must be clear that the England of today is culturally a very different place from the England of 1960.

Now the importance of schools in this changing environment is clearly very great. For one thing, schools get the citizens before anyone else — they go to school before they go to work; we in education have been dealing with UK-born blacks and Asians for a long time, despite the rest of society's perverse adherence to the term 'immigrant'. And to add to the problem, we can say that schools are a repository of traditional English attitudes — about authority, for instance, and about the value of continuity and custom. What will the Asian pupil — or for that matter the Singhalese or the Hong Kong Chinese — make of the panoply of English secondary school life, with its uniform regulations and assumptions about what is good manners and what is not? At the very simple, basic level, what happens to a rigid and long-enforced rule about showering after gym when you start to get pupils with turbans? Presumably something happens to the school and its rules. Equally important, presumably something happens to the home lives of the pupils concerned.

The ideal person to discuss the multi-cultural dimension is Carlton Duncan. He is deputy-head of Sidney Stringer School and Community College in Coventry and is himself of West Indian origin. As a West

Indian in a position of authority in education he is, of course, exceptional. There are few enough teachers from ethnic groups, let alone heads and deputies. His experience and his message are clear — that 'multicultural' means just that. It does not mean that all pupils have to be treated alike, but that each cultural group has to be treated fairly on its own terms. One very interesting discussion point which will inevitably arise from Duncan's writing is what you do about a cultural practice or belief which seems to Western eyes unfair or repressive. Should a school, for example, support the wishes of Asian parents in their desire to segregate adolescent girls from boys? Just what are, or should be, parental rights in such cases? Issues like this will be of more and more importance in our profession in the coming years, and teachers and aspirants should at least be aware of them and have started to formulate the basis for personal belief and practice.

Discipline and the Multi-cultural School

CARLTON DUNCAN

In the final analysis discipline must be assessed in terms of the rule structure of a given institution. The traditional school sometimes unwittingly creates for itself a hoard of disciplinary problems in its over-zealous attempt to foster too many rules. Pregnant with worth though they may appear, it is not only possible for some institutions to survive without many of the rules which they set themselves, but in many cases results will be much more in accord with the disciplinary goals sought earnestly by the institutions.

It is not here suggested that rules and regulations should be relinquished in schools; far from it. Man when he reaches the perfection of virtue is the best of all animals; but if he goes his way without rules and justice he becomes the worst of all brutes. For man unlike other animals has the weapon of reason with which to exploit his base desires and cruelty, and at no time is there more evidence of this than during his school days.

The contention is that, too often the pendulum is swung too far in the opposite direction with undesirable yet avoidable consequences. Many schools, for example, spend an inordinate amount of resources in standardising the apparel worn by their pupils and persuading them to rise to their feet on the expected or unexpected entry of staff or strangers into the classroom. What they actually achieve, in terms of education or discipline, hardly justifies the expenditure.

Similarly, the disciplinary outcome in some schools would be greatly improved if half the efforts directed to containing pupils within the confines of the school's four walls and on regimentally discouraging pupils in their use of unsupervised rooms at recess times were diverted to instructions in the proper and safe usage of the public thoroughfare and in the constructive and beneficial management of their own school premises. Positive guidelines usually outweigh their negative counterparts in terms of results.

The school which thus endeavours to establish an optimum of rules which reflect sound positive thinking is well on its way to achieving that degree of social order which lends itself readily to an atmosphere of learning and creativity.

The typical multi-racial school in England is probably that found in urban and industrial areas which, for obvious reasons, are sources of attraction to the lower working class indigenous whites as well as to Irish, Asian and West Indian immigrants. It is no longer unusual, for example, to find a school with over two-thirds of its pupil population split evenly between Asians and West Indians. These people like all others will have their own peculiar values and beliefs deeply inculcated. Their thoughts and practices will vary enormously depending on their own background.

This cultural multiplicity provides a fertile breeding ground for some interesting conflicts which, if not handled carefully, would lead to disastrous consequences for the school and the disciplinary goals it sets itself. Mannerisms in styles of dress, eating habits, religious practices and attitudes to coeducation are but a few examples. Yet the skilled and thoughtful technician or tactician can derive social order from the most diverse mixture of human beings.

It is not to be assumed that all multi-cultural schools are characterised by this neat three-way split in racial or cultural composition. Quite often one particular race accounts for as much as seventy per cent of the school's population. This fact, where it exists, can be a significant factor in setting the overall disciplinary tone. For better or for worse it aids conformity under group pressure. The disciplinarian has his task made easier or more difficult accordingly. Consider, for example, a multi-cultural school where the predominant sector is Asian. One can expect little resistance from these pupils in enforcing the kind of social order deemed worthwhile and necessary in the school. They are from a background of very rigid discipline where the authority of teachers and elders should never be questioned or disobeyed. There are, of course, arguments against this unquestioning attitude, but its disciplinary advantages cannot be denied. Other pupils who have the opposite attitude stand out prominently. But in time all but a few strong individuals will yield to the way of the majority. Group dynamics can be subtler and more powerful than the cane. For a variety of reasons the same might not be said of schools where indigenous whites or West Indians predominate.

Social scientists have gone to great lengths to establish some sort of correlation between the child's behaviour and its home environment. Poor behaviour and learning difficulties are supposed to be indicative of bad housing and broken or one-parent families. There is no doubt that there is some evidence for this, but the number of boys and girls from such backgrounds who nevertheless maintain exemplary academic and disciplinary records is high enough to cast doubt on the relationship. Serious respect should be shown to the endeavours of the social scientists, but it might be wise to heed Mr Justice Frankfurter who once said 'Sociologists should be on tap, but not on top.'

But for the multi-cultural school the cultural norms of family life will have clear implications for discipline. The white indigenous child is often given greater freedom of mind and individuality than his Asian and West Indian counterparts. The English girl, for example, from sixteen onwards will find it far easier to have evenings out at the local discotheque, youth club, parties and so on. A 'telling off' is regarded as serious and is a very effective means of social control in white homes. Reason rather than authority is made the foundation of discipline. The school is expected to reflect this attitude. Evidence of this expectation might be found in the comparatively high proportion of white parents who are quite willing to lend support to their children in questioning the school's authority. Evidence of the conformity to expectation might be drawn out of the fact that over the last decade or so more and more local authorities and schools have voted against the use of the cane. This humanitarian and reasonable approach to social order is not confined to the homes and the schools. It is an attitude which has been making ground in all corners of society for several years. Even the courts have become increasingly dependent upon social medicine as opposed to punitive measures. The traditionalists have recognised this in their label 'the permissive society'.

Regrettably there are still a number of white homes which actively and quite openly encourage hostility against immigrants; it is thus not surprising when children from these homes become agents for their parents' illwill to others. Potential manifestation of such illwill may range from passive non-recognition of immigrants, through non-cooperation with them to outright insults and physical violence.

In both Asian and West Indian homes there is a very strong tendency for reason to come second to authority. Children lead a rigidly disciplined life, or at least are expected to lead one. Reasoning with children, or simply telling them off, is a rare occurrence. Resort is made to the rod of correction much more frequently than in white homes. The rod is an acceptable way of life in the distant lands from which these people originated. Children accept it and there is no question of resentment or prolonged hatred as some might fear. In fact there is as deep and settled love between parents and children as can be experienced in any other family grouping. It must be admitted that the true immigrant child is rapidly disappearing from the classrooms of this country, but children born in this country of immigrant parents are first exposed to the cultural values shared by their immediate family and it is a long time before the values inculcated in early years become shaken through exposure to more lax and perhaps more attractive values.

The result of all this is that immigrant children often speak with their parents' voices and see with their parents' eyes, not daring to express their own views. Asian and West Indian girls encounter a taboo on evening or night events; and the large majority of these girls simply obey and do not even desire an evening out. All this is the direct result of the principle that children should be seen and not heard.

Immigrant parents expect the school to be as rigid with their children as they would themselves. The school's authority should never be questioned except to remind them of their duty to be rigid and severe with pupils. Clear evidence of this is seen in the fact that immigrant parents find it most difficult to understand reports that their children misbehave at school. Their first question to the teacher is 'Why haven't you caned him/her?' West Indian immigrants in particular will alarm you with stories of how they might have been caned as many as two or three times for arriving one minute late at school in their own days in their country of origin. I myself, for example, during my school days in Jamaica, had the misfortune, one morning on the way to school, to be caught playing marbles by a total stranger who suspected that I might have been missing minutes from school. For this little escapade I was treated to six strokes of the stranger's belt. I arrived at school some six minutes later than I might have been had it not been for the encounter with the stranger, and as the headmaster's policy was one stroke of the cane for every minute late I again collected another six strokes. Folly and fear that a later discovery by my parents would be interpreted to mean the more heinous act of deceit made me disclose the day's beatings to my parents. They showed their sympathy by promptly giving me a sound thrashing for being so mischievous in the first place. This tale is typical and emphasises the rigid discipline which is characteristic of a West Indian society.

Traditional approaches to discipline in British schools cannot then suffice in a situation which proffers such diverse behavioural expectation and practices. Teachers who fail or refuse to notice this diversity will soon give up or draw erroneous conclusions about immigrants. The good intentions should not be mistaken in the all too often heard declarations from teachers in multi-cultural schools to the effect that they will not use the cane; that they will treat all pupils equally; that to them all pupils are alike whatever their colour, religion or background. But the idea of impartiality in such circumstances is unfortunately compatible with very great inequity.

West Indian pupils regard this approach to discipline as easy and permissive and react to it differently from Asians. There is some hint of a 'let's make the most of it, this can't be true' attitude from West Indian pupils. The Asians, however, remain passive, quiet and cooperative. For this reason the West Indian child is often labelled as disruptive, anti-social, aggressive and incorrigible. Passivity fixes the Asian in the 'goody goody' class, a fact which indirectly does him serious injustice and causes him difficulties in other respects.

The West Indians' physical presence (they are often bigger than their Asian and white peers) and their exuberant nature place them squarely in line for these mostly unfair labellings. Their natural exhibitionist and happy-go-lucky attitude to life in general coupled with what is essentially a warm, friendly, perhaps too friendly, and trusting disposition are the factors which largely explain the way West Indians are perceived and consequently mislabelled.

Asians (whether Moslems, Hindus or Sikhs) are of a much more religious disposition – highly conscious of the way they behave, the food they eat, and the clothing they wear. Whilst there is clear evidence that Asians are increasingly rejecting particular aspects of their cultural heritage it might be said with authority that they seldom stray far from their religious tenets. Compared with their West Indian counterparts, the Asians might be considered introverts, but in reality they are simply much more observant and cautious of their immediate circumstances.

Another important factor influencing the distinction in perception of West Indians and Asians arises out of the fact that the Asians have in most cases managed to maintain the extended family pattern in spite of their immigrant status. The newly married, for example, will nearly always start life with their in-laws. Elder brothers and sisters, and sometimes strangers, exercise as much authority over the young as would their parents. The Asian culture is thus very strong in their homes and communities. In fact it is sometimes argued that the immigrant Asian is more Asian in his ways than those he left behind as he still labours in the belief that life in the homeland is as he remembers it some twenty or so years back; never giving countenance to the inevitability of social change, slow though it might be. A responsible member of the family is always at home to give guidance to the young where the family is structured along extended lines. Home-school links are therefore more realistic and the Asian child knows this and behaves accordingly.

But for West Indian immigrants, economic circumstances compel a change in family pattern. They adapt themselves to the nuclear structure. This seldom, if ever, permits an adult to be always at home. This fact weakens cultural pressures and affords little or no opportunity for the home and the school to cooperate. Some West Indian children are likely to exploit this weakness to their later loss and regret.

The very fact that pupils of different racial and cultural backgrounds are brought together is enough to produce disciplinary problems in the school. Preconceptions, stereotyping, ignorance, and insecurity are seedlings of conflict between the different races; and if adults show ineptitude in handling these delicate matters, perfection can hardly be expected from the youngsters.

Many a playground fight is the direct result of racial prejudices, which also engender prolonged tension and hatred in the school. At the same time it must be admitted that a 'chip on the shoulder' attitude is just as likely to cause problems for the school. Here the Asians are apt to come off worst. The quiet and withdrawn frequently attract attacks on themselves. The West Indians' apparently aggressive attitude and their violent temper when under attack minimise the frequency of attacks on them.

An interesting observation in this respect is that whites and West Indians sometimes join forces in harassing Asians. Possible explanations of this strange alliance could be due to the Asians insistence on being seen as 'brown' and not black, which is a term they feel should apply only to Negroes, regardless of the fact that the consequences of being 'brown' or 'black' are the same in reality. The Asians illustrate this point well in that they readily discriminate against Negroes and openly manifest a desire to be considered white. Not finding acceptance in white societies they opt for brown isolation rather than alliance with Negroes except in rather desperate situations. Negroes naturally resent this attitude and therefore find it hard to show sympathetic understanding. Further, there seems to be a great deal more in common between whites and West Indians than between whites and Asians. For example, black music (blues, reggae, jazz) seem to find ready acceptance amongst white discotheque and club-going youths, blacks are seen and known to contribute considerably to the sports and showbusiness fields, all of which are popular with white youths; West Indian carnivals seem to be a great source of attraction for whites; and there appears to be a greater degree of marital integration between whites and black than between whites and brown.

A full appreciation of these intricate matters is essential for the disciplinary structure of the multi-cultural school.

There are certain other matters which are peculiar to Asians and the disciplinarian will do well to get fully acquainted with them. The dieting habits of the Asian child could be the source of disciplinary problems in the school's dining hall. The Sikhs, for example, will not eat beef and the Moslems will not eat pork. Asian girls are usually expected to keep their legs covered. The school's physical education programmes will need to make adjustments and allowances on the question of dress for physical education activities if conflicts both with pupils and with their parents are to be avoided.

To facilitate the proper functioning of the institution of arranged marriages certain obligations are placed upon the Asian family system. Very serious social consequences would result from non-observation of these obligations. From the age of puberty the Asian female should not fraternise with the opposite sex. This is to ensure that she remains a virgin until marriage. The Asian family which fails to observe this requirement may never find husbands for the daughters of the family.

This has some serious implications for the disciplinary structure of the multi-cultural school. To begin with the family transfers this responsibility to the school for five or more days per week. It becomes an enormously difficult task for the school to separate the sexes (even if it accepted this responsibility) for one race and to allow or encourage togetherness with other races.

An increasing number of Asian girls are rebelling against this aspect of their culture. They seek various avenues of escape, ranging from outright and open defiance of parents and teachers who try to keep them culture bound, through running away from home and truancy from school to attempted suicide even in school. The repercussions for the school's disciplinary structure can be enormous.

Scheming Asian boys, knowing the full pressures the girls are under, have used moral blackmail to introduce further disciplinary problems. A usual trick is to get the girls to the park for a photograph. The girl is photographed next to a boy and from then on she must do as the boy (or in some cases, boys) suggests under threat of the photograph being released to her parents. An upward movement in the school's internal truancy figures is usually a good indicator that problems of this nature exist.

Many Asian girls lose their motivation to do well academically as soon as they near school leaving age. They know only too well that emphasis from then on will be on preparation for the marriage market. This loss of motivation usually shows itself in the school's homework organisation. It becomes increasingly difficult to get cooperation from such pupils – motivation is replaced by nonchalance.

One problem of discipline which does not arise too often but which is nevertheless worthy of note is the occasional report from female teachers that Asian boys, especially Moslems, do not accept discipline from women teachers. Historically most societies either consciously or sub-consciously subordinated their women. (This is what the Women's Liberation Movement is about.) Asian societies are no exception to this. If anything they appear to be greater perpetrators of this practice. In systems where it is still possible to practice polygamy, where the need to give women equal educational opportunities is played down, where single-sex schools are still highly valued and where high offices are reserved for the male, it is to be expected that female authority will be resented. The multi-cultural school must expect these problems and find disciplinary solutions to them.

The wars between the Sikhs and Moslems may have ceased but the wounds and scars are sometimes still carried by the different communities. Unfortunately the young usually learn a biased account of the past and this is often at the root of playground fights between young Asian boys of different religious beliefs.

Finally, where English is the child's second language the teacher may experience difficulty in controlling disciplinary problems via the medium of sarcasm, which can be a very effective measure where it is fully understood. In addition language difficulties may result in the child's failure to understand orders or instructions, and thus what appears to be disobedience is really non-comprehension. This point does not apply exclusively to the Asian sector of the multi-cultural school, but is most marked there. Although most West Indians' mother tongue is English, their language of verbal communication is vastly different from the Queen's English. Hence, the West Indian child, like his Asian colleague, but to a lesser extent, may find himself not reacting appropriately to instructions, orders or sarcasms through simple misunderstandings.

The answers for coping with these various problems will not simply be a question of making the appropriate exceptions where the rules and regulations of the school are in conflict with cultural demands or expectation. Indeed, making exceptions could lead to greater problems for the school. Children are observant but do not understand readily; and they react sensitively in a negative manner to what they regard as prejudicial to their interests. For this reason alone the multi-cultural school must be in constant search for measures which discriminate positively but which are just – and seen to be just – to all its pupils.

We have seen how external forces such as foreign culture, the family and community expectations can influence the disciplinary structure of the multi-cultural school. We must now consider the effect of educational policy decisions and the internal organisation of the school itself.

It will be admitted that the school which is highly motivated academically is also less riddled with disciplinary problems. The simple explanation is that the more effort and energy spent on pursuing matters which attract social and institutional approbation, the less there is for trouble making. Important factors in building and maintaining motivation are self-identity and self-esteem. Where these are lacking in any significant degree the school's motivation suffers, and truancy, class disruptiveness, conflicts between pupils, bullying, teacher-pupil conflicts, abuse and misuse of language, graffiti, vandalism, violence and theft become rife.

It is an unfortunate fact that in some multi-cultural schools, albeit unwittingly, the white-orientated system is causing black children to view themselves as inferior. This fact is poignantly demonstrated where the black child studying her face in one of the school mirrors was heard to remark 'Ugh, aren't I black'.

The same point is illustrated by the black boy who asked 'Miss, are we allowed to?' when questioned by his Art teacher, in a multi-cultural school, why he did not show some black people in his sketch of a local street scene. Very recently I silently shed a tear when a seventeen-year-old West Indian boy came to me full of profuse apologies for disregarding my request for social order from him at the school's youth gathering the previous evening. It was only after the incident that he had learned that I was one of the Deputy Heads of the school. The last thing he had wanted to do was to defy authority, but his image of the black person did not extend to someone at that level.

What then is wrong in our schools? The bitter truth is that the immigrant children being educated in England today are short of heroes on whom to model their aspirations. Among their people those whom they see readily as achievers are pop singers and sportsmen. Beyond this their aspirations can reach no further than following dad on the buses, or mum as a hospital ward-maid or charwoman. Where are the black teachers? Where are the black heads and deputy heads? If this is significant then there are clear implications for educational staffing policy both at national and local levels. If we eschew the ethics of this situation and concentrate solely on the implications for the school's disciplinary objectives, it is still difficult to deny that what is needed is a sufficiently large number of well trained and able immigrant teachers at all levels in our schools – particularly the multi-cultural ones – to encourage the right self-image and perception of black or brown people.

In some multi-cultural schools the soul-destroying factor for the immigrant child is the school's curriculum. The traditional mono-cultural curriculum lingers on in spite of the changed nature of the school's population. The English, History and Social Science Departments in these schools could work wonders by encouraging a multi-cultural curriculum. The works of such people as Phillis Wheatley, Claude McKay, Paul Laurence Dunbar and Gwendolyn Brooks, could be drawn into literature syllabuses alongside such traditionally recognised authors as Shakespeare, Hardy and Goldsmith, with astounding effect upon the disciplinary order of the school.

The opportunity is there for history departments to put black and white pupils in touch with the likes of Toussaint L'Ouverture, Dessalines and Christophe who fought against the French in Haiti; to enable these pupils to evaluate the work of black politicians and early leaders towards emancipation and so place them in perspective against Wilberforce and Lincoln who for too long have appeared to have achieved this purpose virtually single-handed. Is it not the obligation of our schools to bring to light for all our pupils the achievements of black people in such fields as science and industry, literature, education, politics, religion, music, the theatre and visual art, to mention just a few?

It is most alarming that in some multi-cultural schools with a significantly high proportion of Asians, Christianity is still the only means of religious communication either through 'corporate act of worship' or through academic instructions. Further, in spite of the fact that some examination boards have for years recognised the Asian languages at GCE levels, foreign language options have not advanced beyond Spanish, German and French. This act of alienation of the immigrant child through non-recognition of his culture, his language, his religion – in short, his make-up – can have only a negative effect on the discipline of the school.

It could be very productive in disciplinary terms if, when arrangements are being considered for the annual festivities such as the school's Christmas Pantomime, some thoughts were given to celebration of Diwali or Guru Nanak's birthday. Similarly, a school's concert programme might well give its West Indian pupils a chance to exercise their skills in creole and to demonstrate their rhythmic and musical qualities. These may appear to the reader to be rather trivial matters but their pay-off is of enormous worth to the ethos of the school.

Racial and religious prejudices are present in society generally, and it would be naive to consider that the teaching profession is not affected by this malignancy. To the extent that it does affect the profession it may well be a negative disciplinary factor. Children are astute in identifying their enemies and are unlikely to lend cooperation to those they mistrust even where such mistrusted ones are bearers of the school's seal and letters of conduct. Further, a concomitant of prejudice is scorn, and psychologically this may be a source of reinforcement of the feeling of inadequacy in the minds of young persons. The warning then is that the attitude of staff to pupils can be counter-productive. Children of a multi-cultural background cannot be treated as if they were all alike but they must be treated with fairness.

Identity erosion begins very early on in the immigrant child's school life. A comparatively high proportion of West Indian children find themselves in ESN schools mainly on account of their linguistic incapabilities. Unfortunately for West Indians, the tests used for categorising pupils thus early in life will be culture-biased against them, since whether or not the West Indian child was born in this country the dominant language experience which he will have had will be creole in nature. Then the old psychologically founded adage of living up to expectation will apply.

At secondary school level, categorisation takes a different form. It is still common to find schools in which streaming, banding and setting are still the norm. This is done in some schools along very rigid lines. At the end of the third year in school certain pupils are destined through selection to sit the more favoured GCE, others, less able, will sit Mode One CSEs and the least able will sit Mode Three CSEs (a misuse, in fact of Mode Three).

Immigrant pupils in schools which practise mixed ability teaching are more likely to sample the GCEs than their counterparts in streamed schools since they will have had an additional two years in which to overcome some of the cultural difficulties they must encounter. But quite often in the streamed schools many immigrants are relegated to the Mode Three ranks from which they will never escape. In a recent discussion, the Headmistress of one of these schools pointed out that the child has a further chance at GCEs in the Sixth Form. This might be so, but the worry is about the number of wasted human beings who simply become disciplinary problems because their hopes and aspirations have become dissipitated by the school's organisation.

The final episode of this erosion of identity is met in the employment market, where ostensibly the means of selection is examination certificates. At least this is so if you are an immigrant and have none. However, for those immigrants who do have examination certificates the basis of selection can sometimes quickly change to one of colour. The immigrant child is then left with a feeling of worthlessness – of being cheated and at odds with the system. It is no wonder that many will turn to crime and wretchedness in the wider society. The previous years of indiscipline and confrontation with authority will now aid development along these lines.

Finally, teacher expectation is as pertinent to discipline and academic achievement as are the school's staffing composition and its curriculum.

Too often one comes across the view that Asians are too ambitious – 'They all want to be brain surgeons.' The implication here is that they are stepping beyond their bounds, forgetting, perhaps, the dependency of our Health Service on Asian medical men and women. West Indians are considered good sportsmen and sports women; fun-loving, but not likely to do well academically. There is evidence that often such judgements, expectations and relegations are undertaken with genuine belief in their appropriateness. This might be so but there is a chance of serious errors which can be psychologically disastrous, and the full extent of the disaster cannot be measured until the immigrants' competitive weaknesses are called in question in the employment and further educational markets.

One of the dangers of having a low expectation of pupils is that there is a tendency to design programmes which accord with the expectations. When pupils are not stretched to capacity they accept an invitation to restlessness. My own experience over the years is that all children can be encouraged to perform at a high level provided they are made to feel that if others can do it, so can they. High-level performance is commensurate with a better self-image and hence greater motivation and sounder discipline.

A man will be a better teacher as he will be a better architect or physician, if his mind is open to the movement of thoughts on the profounder issues of life, beyond his immediate professional concerns. If his mind is so open, he can hardly fail to have some sort of philosophy of his own. It is this lust for learning added to willingness to depart from traditional measures which is largely responsible for the success of teachers in establishing social order in schools such as Sidney Stringer School and Community College with its 54 per cent Asians, 38 per cent whites, 6 per cent West Indians plus another 2 per cent Chinese and others composing its 1200-plus pupils.

At Stringer the password is care; and care is genuine only where it takes account of what the recipient feels and thinks.

There is a close tie-up with the community which the school serves. Community support and cooperation will continue to flow only where the community is able to identify with the institution. At Stringer identification becomes possible through the school's staffing composition. Ten members of the teaching staff are Asian and so are a few others in non-teaching capacities. The author is one of the school's three Deputy Heads.

Just over two years ago a Director of Multi-cultural studies was appointed at scale four level, his main function being to ensure that the various departments and faculties in the school mounted an adequate multi-cultural studies programme. Programmes to public examinations level are mounted in Asian Studies: as well as French, German and Russian, Hindi, Punjabi and Gujarati are also available as options for foreign language studies.

This kind of communal atmosphere, once estabished, sets the scene where everyone within it is developing simultaneously. Each person's development is affected by and influences that of the next. Everyone within the system must feel keen to achieve worthy personal standards. Personal examples on matters of taste, attitude to work, attitude to people and property become exemplary and are in fact copied.

There is then little or no place for a punitive system to

extract what is deemed to be desirable from our fellow men. Naturally, there will be some need for constant vigilance – not in a policing sense – moved by a sense of genuine interest in the suitable development of all in all respects, vigilance through dialogue, praise, example and disapprobation of the anti-social. When all around us feel this sense of identity, worthwhileness and security then we are achieving.

Yet it is possible to find a large multi-cultural school with over half its 1600 pupils West Indians and another third Asian, where every picture or poster adorning the school's drab walls portrays a white face; where teachers are all white; where the cane is the only means, though ineffective, of social control; where a multi-cultural curriculum however modest would be quickly rejected as thoroughly divisive; where the mono-cultural curriculum will be justified in terms of public policy. But public policy is a restive horse and once you get astride it there is no knowing where it will take you.

6

A constant theme in this book is that pupils in school are human beings with rights as well as responsibilities. While our writers span a tremendous breadth of educational and social philosophies, they are agreed on the need to treat children with concern and care. In English education this view has, I suppose, always been most strongly epitomised in the way that sixth formers are treated. Quite commonly, once a pupil is into the sixth form he is subject to a totally different sort of regime. He may, for instance, be allowed to wear different clothes from his younger brethren. He may have much freer use of the school building. He may be able to come and go much as he pleases. There will also be at least some freedom to plan his own work. The senior pupil, it is thought, can think for himself, and deserves to be given freedom and responsibility in amounts suited to his more adult status.

What Henry Pluckrose is saying in the chapter which follows, is that this sort of freedom and trust can be extended to all pupils; that all children thrive on trust and participation. He drives a coach and horses through a number of the assumptions which are at the root of time-honoured practices in our junior schools. The idea, for instance, that children must be chased out of the building when no adult is present to supervise them; or that they are not to be trusted with expensive equipment unless a teacher is present, and perhaps not even then. What makes his thoughts so valuable, of course, is that he writes not as an ivory tower theoretician, but as a man who practises what he preaches, as head of a city primary school.

The Caring School

HENRY PLUCKROSE

Order

The only lecture that I can remember from my college days which touched upon order and discipline began with an exhortation, biblical in its intensity, to 'consider for a moment the problems of the public convenience'. I forget exactly what followed, but the talk remains fixed in my memory. The speaker, a senior lecturer in the education department, laid great emphasis upon the need to encourage people to respect public property as if it were their own. 'No one,' he remarked, 'would treat their own toilet as they do those in the King's Road.'

I tell this story because it brings into sharp focus (although somewhat obliquely) the central use of discipline in school. If the school building and the equipment, furniture, books and material it houses are regarded by pupils as property for which they need show little responsibility, a climate is established which, if not actually encouraging vandalism and disorder, offers little positive support for the development of a more positive, caring approach by all who use it.

My first observation, then, is that schools ought to be places which identify with children and their needs. If, however, the school is seen as a place which is governed by petty rules which bear no relationship to the real world, then many children will quickly come to regard school as an alien environment. If these rules are rigorously enforced (as they surely must be if the rules and those who design and impose them are to maintain any credibility) then the alienation is extended still further.

Let me examine this with a specific example, one which

applies to the majority of our schools. For apparently sound reasons a rule is made that children are to be excluded from their classrooms unless their teachers are present. The underlying assumption, unspoken yet unequivocally clear, is that children cannot be trusted unless they are supervised and that the school building, the classrooms and corridors are places which children enter only on adult sufferance. In these circumstances the teaching staff must be regarded as janitors.

This example applies to both primary and secondary schools. In the school in which I currently work, all the children (be they five or eleven years old) are allowed into school when they arrive. They are expected to respect the school fabric, because to behave otherwise would be the exceptional thing to do. The school my daughter attends has quite a different approach. Students are allowed into the building when they have reached the fifth secondary year. The rule is arbitrary and lacks logic. An ill-behaved fifteen-year-old may enter unsupervised, whilst a twelve-year-old who is trustworthy is excluded. In such circumstances personal responsibility is discouraged. Trust dispensed so illogically is hardly likely to be regarded seriously by those to whom it is given.

Discipline (or lack of it) stems, in home, school, office and factory, from the hidden, unspoken patterns which are established by the dominant members of the group. A child who regards teachers as adults who enforce unrealistic and unreasonable regulations is hardly likely to regard school as an institution with which she can identify. If (to carry the example developed above still further) children must remain out of doors in the bitterest weather while teachers shelter in the warm, the common humanity which binds adult and child is put severely under strain. When, as sometimes happens, the relationship cracks, the school is seen as the teacher's castle, an institution which deserves attack, both overtly and by subterfuge.

This feeling, for it is difficult to describe in a more exact term, has been described as the 'ethos' of a school. If each child can be made to feel that, though shared with all who use it, the school is also their own (on a personal rather than collective level) discipline/order/control is less likely to require an authoritarian presence to enforce it.

The 'ethos', or spirit of a school, cannot be established overnight. It must be based on the real participation of all who live and work within it. There needs to be a clear policy on the part of the teaching staff on how to encourage the responsible use of school equipment, how to correct offenders, how to develop each child's self respect and sense of personal integrity. In turn these ideals need to be shared with the other adults working in the school, for an evenness of approach is essential. To have your excuse for lateness accepted by your teacher (for example) only to have it dismissed as a pack of lies by the school secretary will understandably provoke resentment. It might also undermine many weeks of effort on the part of the teacher who has been attempting to show a recalcitrant and reluctant child that school is a caring institution worthy of his trust and support.

In this respect the role of parents must not be forgotten. We who teach cannot deal with an ill-disciplined child without the cooperation of the home. Self-responsibility and self-discipline (the goal of all schools since the days of Sparta) cannot develop if home and school are so out of sympathy that neither attempts to understand the other.

Some twenty years ago I taught in a school to which children came bruised from the beatings they had received at home. I could, with little difficulty, have extended this regime to my classroom. Although a child who respected the tyrant at home would surely understand a tyrant at school, I tried to be gentle. I was not always successful and often despaired. Looking back I wonder whether I would have dared to beat Norman as hard as his father did. If I scored less in the violence stakes, I would merely have shown myself to be 'soft'; at least when I talked to him I was projecting a different approach. My meetings with Norman's parents, which were short, sharp and, from my point of view depressing, did serve one useful purpose. They gave me the opportunity to indicate other ways of controlling children, to suggest that quiet consistency and the odd word of praise might achieve more than physical conflict. It would be pleasant to present the personal experience as a story of success. Eventually Norman (and his younger brother Robert whom I also taught) both went to prison. On their release they came to see me, not to beg or to ask for help, simply to talk. Did this, I sometimes wonder, suggest that when these lads became fathers their children could hope for more understanding parents than they had?

With the parents of the school in which I work, I regularly attempt to explain our aims, the reason for our treating children as we do, as reasonable, responsible, cooperative creatures who have a thirst for learning and who want to cooperate and be trusted. If this can spill over into homes where the view is quite different (i.e. that children are essentially lazy, thoughtless and self-centred) then so much the better. If the home view remains unaltered, then at the very least we can show children (as I did to Norman and Robert) that brutality and authoritarianism are not the only path.

The third element we need to consider is the child himself. No learning programme (and discipline in school often falls apart because the child fails to identify with it) is going to be effective unless those taking part have a clear idea of the role they have to play.

At the school in which I work we allow children to enter school at any reasonable time. We therefore expect them to use this privilege responsibly. They do. Since we allow them access to expensive tools and equipment, we expect them to handle them with care. By and large they do. Since we argue that the school is a big enough place to accommodate all who want to come, we assume that the petty squabbles which so often characterise school life rarely need occur. If it is mature to recognise that not everybody likes everybody else, then conflicts which stem from personality clashes can be resolved without resort to violent words or deeds. They are.

I am not for one moment suggesting that we have no problems. Of course we lose the odd hammer, of course Brendon sometimes is less than kind to Mary and Peter is not as dedicated to his Maths work when he comes to school early to complete it as he might be. What I am suggesting, however, is that in the process of growing, of learning self-control, of becoming socially responsible beings, children will make mistakes. These mistakes need to be corrected in an environment which is supportive and sensitive to their needs. To argue that all mistakes must be ruthlessly punished is to ignore the growth which comes from self-correction, from admitting an error, from being accepted back into a community even though for a moment there has been a failure to live up to its standards.

Alongside this, I also believe it important to involve pupils (even quite young ones) in decision making. This again takes two forms. The first is to establish within the school a small council elected by the children themselves. This council discusses with me some of the more traditional areas of discipline within the school, from sweet papers in the playground to the most suitable method of retrieving footballs that are on the school roof. The second and more important aspect is to programme the school so that a proportion of the work is completed individually. There are many times a week when children work under the direction of teachers. There are also many times when a child is given the responsibility to complete work. Do I finish my Maths now or my English? Do I attempt some more weaving, add to my painting or write up the account of yesterday's school trip? Is this so very different from the mother who has to decide whether at a particular moment of the day to go shopping, do the washing, bake a cake, repair a dress or watch her favourite serial on TV?

It seems to me that order in school does not stem from the minority group (i.e. the teachers) issuing rules which are subsequently enforced with verbal stick, lightened with the occasional smile and word of praise.

If schools are to be orderly places (and I think they must be) then our aim should be to design a 'life style' which is comprehensible to the children who are attending the school, is appropriate to their age and interests and *can be seen to be* reasonable. I make this last point because so often conflicts within school flare up when petty rules are unthinkingly enforced. Let me illustrate this with an example. The children who deliberately wore plimsolls to school against the publicly expressed wishes of their headteacher were not really complaining about a school rule, but against the lack of sympathy which had been shown to one of their number who had been suspended for being improperly dressed. Subsequent enquiries showed that the boy, who came from a very poor home, had either to wear plimsolls to school or attend in bare feet.

This is an extreme example and to give undue weight to such incidents is both unwise and unhelpful. Somewhere between the extremes of unquestioned adult authority and unfettered childhood freedom there lies the balance which all who work with young people should seek to attain. There will, of necessity, be some sanctions, sanctions which are understood by the pupils and their parents. But these sanctions will have sufficient flexibility to deal with every case on its merits.

My argument then is a simple one. Believing as I do that 'curriculum is everything that goes on within a school', I would suggest that in undertaking a review of discipline within any institution teachers and parents need first to look at the school programme as a whole. Is it satisfying the basic needs of children and young people? Is it humane? Does it handle difficult children with sensitivity? Are such rules as are made reasonable and necessary for the safety of the individual and all who work within the institution? Are sanctions appropriate? Do they respect the intelligence and integrity of the young people, or are they meaningless chores?

It might be, of course, that this is the very point that my lecturer was trying to make. If schools are places where corporate responsibility is rarely emphasised, where writing as an activity has little personal relevance, where the individual is lost in the crowd, then perhaps the condition of the toilets in the King's Road still contains a hidden message for us all.

7

School is a place where people talk and where learning is conducted through the medium of language. This much is obvious, and in recent years a very great deal has been said and written about 'language and learning'. Gradually teachers have come to realise that language is not just a neutral vehicle for ideas but has a life and importance of its own.

It seemed to me, in planning this book, that language was a crucial element in discipline. After all 'telling pupils what to do' is an important part of the traditional disciplinary relationship. Clearly, one way into examining the relationship was through the language used, and it seemed clear to me also that a discussion of this kind would be bound to broaden out and encompass all aspects of the pupil-teacher relationship.

Peter Woods of the Open University has, rather to my satisfaction, proved that language is crucial, and that when you follow the linguistic theme along, you find that it can be used as a key with which to enter, and gain another perspective upon, such things as the nature of the difference between various teaching styles.

The Language of Order

PETER WOODS

There is no magic recipe for classroom order, any more than there is for 'successful teaching'. It would be difficult to get a generally acceptable view of what such states entail. Is a quiet class, apparently dutifully writing or listening to teacher, necessarily showing good order? Has a child who has misbehaved, been scolded, and now sits still and silent, been successfully disciplined? Is the whole school, in Assembly, neatly arranged in forms and years, bowing their heads to say the Lord's Prayer, singing the hymn, listening to the announcements, filing in and out in twos, an 'ordered' gathering? The truth might be the opposite of appearances. The class might be doing something entirely different from that required by the teacher. The scolded child might be smouldering with resentment awaiting the first opportunity for revenge. And the Assembly, though going through some of the forms, may be far away in spirit, and indeed under cover of the mass appearance, indulging in all manner of local illicit pastimes.

Further, what constitutes order for one teacher is not necessarily the same for another. Though the standard model is still suffused with elements of the Protestant Ethic, such as quietness, paying attention, respect for authority, obeying rules, and preparedness to work hard, the introduction of progressive forms of teaching during the last decade, together with certain developments in society with which they were associated and affecting authority relationships at large, has opened up this model, and in some instances posed a contrary view. It might be construed as an external-internal dichotomy. In the former, the work, the rules, the authority are all external to the pupil, and the teacher relies on the pupil's sense of duty in meeting their requirements. In the latter, these very elements do not exist as separate entities, because they are internalised by the pupil. Rules are 'negotiated' so that norms of behaviour are established through practice, and common understandings arrived at. 'Work' is not always hard labour, imposed from without, but creative and joyful, and self-motivated. And 'authority' is simply not an issue, never has to be appealed to, because relationships are founded on mutual and equal trust and respect.

The outward forms of these two styles – posed here as ideal types – are mutually conflicting. What is order for one, is chaos for the other. Their associated vocabularies and forms of communication reflect this gulf. It is not difficult to pick out examples of the traditional/authoritarian style:

> 'Quiet now! Sit down. Get out your books.'
> 'Hands on heads! Eyes closed!'
> 'The whole class will be kept in unless the person owns up!'
> 'We can tell you what to do because you're in our care. We're teachers and you're pupils.'

The last example reveals an 'open' traditional technique, involving an attempt to explain the rationale to pupils, which of course offends the purest authoritarian style. For attempts at explanation are concessions that ultimately might undermine authority. Interestingly, the purest style probably involves little speech at all, but has become so routinised that the most minimal cues serve as indicators – the teacher's appearance for the class to stand, a simple hand movement for them to sit, a glance to forestall a suspected deviation. At the other extreme it is marked by much shouting, nagging, moaning, or the teacher 'getting on to you', urging, giving orders. The initiative of the classroom is one-sided, there is no discourse, except in the teacher's terms. It may feature sarcasm, ridicule, showing-up.

However, the 'silent-cue' authoritarian is becoming rarer. The same social forces that promoted progressive styles have wrung concessions from the traditional. The 'shouting' mode above – all too common, especially in secondary schools – is a backs-to-the-wall technique, forced by pupil pressure, and opting for an impositional style in a (usually) vain attempt to restore 'silent-cue' conditions. Others opt for a form of indulgence, coaxing within an authoritarian mode. Such forms of speech may be marked by occasional explanation (as above), by appeals that emphasise the common venture, by civility such as frequent use of 'please' and 'thank you' and friendliness, marked, for example, by the use of christian names. Such paternalism, however, involves a conditional benevolence, and can revert to nastiness if the implicit contract is breached.

This occasional indulgence in friendliness, civility and equality, strategically incidental in the traditional style, is fundamental to progressive styles. So child-centred language is individually oriented and all-embracing. Matters like 'control', 'discipline', 'work' are not issues. Thus a classroom can seem to be in vast disarray – noisy, with much action, and the teacher not to be seen – but in fact order might prevail. The teacher might be in the midst of the class, talking to individuals as he goes round in a personal way, attending to personal difficulties. The mode of discourse at the individual level is entirely different, of course, from that at the 'class' level, and might be punctuated with personal (complimentary) references to appearance, state of health, family, leisure pursuits. The net result from the class in terms of learning might be greater than from a class of silent pupils.

Thus control is defined differently according to teaching style. To one it is a central issue, to the other not an issue at all. One can only succeed or fail in control therefore in traditional styles, though these practitioners see many forms of progressive teaching as one entire failure. The difference might be illustrated in another way – through roles and contexts. Schools are well established institutions, dealing with masses of children for which, through trial and error, they have developed certain techniques and attitudes. Lumped together, they might be termed the teacher role. In a sense, it is de-individualised and dehumanised, because it is dealing with masses, classes and groups in a fairly mechanical and routinised way. There is a kind of 'teacher talk' through which this role is expressed, which makes frequent reference to the institutional symbols that mark the boundaries of behaviour. Such symbols would be school rules (which govern every aspect of behaviour), school uniform (which governs appearance), the timetable – the 'bell' or periods (which governs permitted activities and structures the school day). Success in gaining control consists in socialising the young into acceptance of the proper meaning of these symbols.

It might also be marked by frequent reference to the functional objectives – examinations, references, occupations. These can be put almost into a separate compartment of life, to do with the public sphere. So that, while some teachers may appear like automatons, or prison wardens, or regimental sergeant-majors, *that* may apply for only official parts of the school day; at other times they may appear completely different. Pupils often remark on the stark contrast between some teachers in lessons and out, in school time or out of school time, when talking to them individually or as a class. Some teachers themselves are often amazed, so easy and 'natural' is it to fall into the teacher role, at the difference in themselves, which they attribute to differences in the pupils. Others intentionally adopt the role with all its accoutrements, quite deliberately and quite entirely. In the sometimes chaotic waters of class control, it helps to draw straight lines – and pupils, at least, 'know where they are'. The synthetic nature of such control – as opposed to evidencing an absolute power relationship – is revealed by the friendly relationships that pertain in off-duty moments. However, it always rankles to some degree, for, as one pupil told me, you cannot like school because 'you can't be yourself'.

Other teachers manage to iron out those boundaries and to keep the activity of teaching within a total conception of life rather than as a separate compartment. They do not assume a separate role, and therefore do not employ role language. They talk to pupils not as pupils (a distinctive role) but as people. In some cases this might almost amount to a joint conspiracy against the school, in that any references to institutional symbols are likely to be critical ones, implying conflict either between the school as an institution and how it constrains and/or misdirects one's natural inclinations, or between a dominant culture and a subsidiary one. Interestingly, this is only a hollow conspiracy, for the allowance for internal criticism and the release of tension together with some teacher support is actually functional for the school and dissipates much incipient discontent. All schools, therefore, should have some teachers who can chat to pupils on their own terms. The requirements of so many of our large secondary schools militate against this. The constraints of resources and numbers, and the requirements of certification force a bureaucratic response. In mainstream subjects, therefore, and in the upper hierarchy, whose job it is to facilitate their teaching, there is little scope for 'person' work.

So far, then, the teacher is faced with two dilemmas – concerning two opposing teaching styles, and role and person. As he watches and listens to other experienced teachers at work, he may witness various combinations of approach, often in the same teacher, who might ring the changes according to class, subject or time of day. Another dilemma is that arising from the cultural divide between teachers and many pupils. If parts of Bernstein's original thesis concerning differences between middle and working-class children's speech has since been hotly contested, there are nonetheless self-evident differences between much teacher and much pupil talk.[1] For a start, there is a vast imbalance of power. Some research has shown, for example, that secondary school teachers talk for seventy per cent of lesson time, and speak three to four times as much as all the class put together. Other studies have shown how teachers keep 'conversational control' over topics. Stubbs calls such language 'metacommunication':

> communication about communication: messages which refer back to the communication system itself, checking whether it is functioning properly. . . . [Teachers] control the channels of communication by opening and closing them: 'OK now listen all of you.' They control the amount of talk by asking pupils to speak or keep quiet: 'Colin, what were you going to say?' They control the content of the talk and define the relevance of what is said: 'Now we don't want any silly remarks.' They control the language focus used: 'That's not English'. And they try to control understanding: 'Who knows what this means?'[2]

Of course this might be more evident in formal lessons, but the same approach to some degree has been noted in comparatively 'progressive' situations.[3]

Another feature of teacher/pupil speech differences is the specialist talk employed by teachers in the classroom. Barnes gives this example of a teacher speaking:

> They were called 'city states' because they were complete in themselves. . . . They were governed by themselves . . . ruled by themselves . . . they supported themselves [short omission] . . . these states were complete in themselves because the terrain between cities was so difficult that it was hard for them to communicate. . . .

Barnes *et al* comment that 'in trying to explain "city states" the teacher seems unable to escape from language equally unfamiliar to children – "complete in themselves", "ruled by themselves", "tended to be" etc'.[4]

On the other hand, pupils in response to teacher 'secondary education talk' will inhibit their own particular forms of linguistic competence, and learn a highly stylised and barren kind of pupil talk. Then again, in their conversations with their peers they sometimes employ language teachers understand only too well, but would prefer not to hear. In fact some teachers find some forms of talk among children hard to take, especially among girls. One teacher recounted to me how one day a group of fifth form girls thought he had left the room, when in fact he was in the store cupboard. 'As 'e gone? Right, I'll tell yer then!' There followed a tale with such lurid sexual details that it made the teacher 'wish a hole would open up and he'd fall down it'. He was 'frightened almost to breathe in case he betrayed his presence' and 'peered through a crack to make sure they'd gone'. This teacher considered himself broadminded, more so, perhaps, than this one:

> They're terrible, particularly the girls, they're revolting, they really are – filthy, vile, despicable. . . . I don't catch what they say, thank God, I just hear the guffaws – you wonder how much is directed at you. . . .

Thus, teachers find it hard to join with pupils in this kind of discussion, or even to witness it. In fact, it is often used as a weapon by pupils in 'confrontational laughter', wherein certain cultural forms, such as 'bad' language, are produced apparently accidentally to shock a teacher and force a submission. Language, then, can be a powerful armament in cultural warfare, particularly in schools where the proprieties of speech and language are a prime concern about which teachers are particularly sensitive. Teachers can hardly join in such conversations, or use such language in class, but there are other forms of less 'unprofessional' culture-identification. Awareness of pupil cultural forms and particularly linguistic styles is a necessary prerequisite for all teachers. Too often, the teacher assumes that he employs a standard mode of discourse to which all pupils roughly approximate, when, in fact, a huge gap exists. If he is aware of these differences and their nature, he will at least know how to differentiate between friendly gesture and intended insult, ordinary pupil discourse and submission. He may also feel able to join them to some extent. One teacher I met captivates a particularly deviant group of boys with a fund of rather risqué jokes, and a lurid descriptive form. For firemen on motorway duties, 'There's nothing like putting your hand in a hot, soggy, palpitating mass of guts to see if you can get a hook in somewhere.'

There is no doubt that this teacher was successful in terms of keeping these boys' interest, teaching them something and 'controlling' them. However, the paradox caused by the teacher having to resolve so many dilemmas, is illustrated by this teacher offending as many pupils in his form as he delighted, particularly girls. 'He only talks to the boys. We can't see the board, or hear him, except when he's being rude sometimes. It's boring, and when we talk we get jumped on. We might only whisper something and he'll be right nasty.'

With the girls he was found to use more authoritarian techniques with, if anything, more of a teacher-pupil gap and more emphasis on teacher power than is customary. 'If you don't stop that silly talking, I'll *ram* your heads together!'

Thus, this teacher with the same class simultaneously employs forms of speech representing the extremes of culture-identification and separation, one relational, one oppositional. It is not difficult to imagine that with the next teacher (and probably most) the roles might be reversed, that is identification with the 'good' girls, and opposition to the 'bad' boys.

Cultural identification does not always work with the bad lads. One might be suspected of the most heinous of crimes – 'creeping' – or one might simply overshoot. A radical teacher I know made little impression on his classes with his attempts to subvert the power basis of the school, his films of Summerhill, his foreign films of freedom, permissiveness and sexual licence – all fronted with a 'libertarian' form of language. This was because they were already partially socialised into the current system and had formed adaptations to cope. Those adaptations now came to form the norm, so that any attempt to subvert their reference point was perceived as an attempt to subvert *them*. One girl opined, 'He's not a proper teacher. He doesn't tell you off.' And a boy commented after a permissive film, 'That stuff's all right in films, but life's not like that, is it?' Where cultural identification is successful it might be resented by other members of staff, who see it as undermining their authoritarian stand, and as essentially defeatist.

So the teacher is faced with cultural differences as well as those of pedagogical style and of role/person. One might also add sexual and generational differences. Talking to girls might take a different form from talking to boys, as with the teacher above, and talking to seven-year-olds is rather different from talking to fifteen-year-olds. Teachers sometimes take a baby-ish attitude towards the latter, which turns the intended censure into self-ridicule. A simple example: 'Stephen, you're a naughty boy!' The use of the early maturational state ('boy') with a behavioural description commonly associated with infants displaces the censure, and removes the whole activity to a plane of reality which can be made light of, incorporated into one's own accommodations.

In other instances, the labels stick, and pupils grow into them. This applies to intelligence as well as behaviour. While on occasions tactics such as the use of baby talk for supposed 'thick' kids might simply earn the contempt of their natural intelligence, on others, the general approach does have an effect: 'We all know you're not the brightest, but if you work hard I'll get you through your CSE's'. The use of such language, especially in conjunction with an authoritarian style, can be self-fulfilling, for 'If they treat us like kids, we'll act like kids.'

In vain might teachers plead, in their turn, that 'If they act like children, we'll treat them like children'. The vicious circle is aided by such language, and in some instances 'control' might not be the intention, so much as revenge or 'scoring points'. Similar misalignments of language occur at the other end of the scale, that is by using terms and tones younger children have no experience of and hence treat as strange and funny. Thus deadly dire and serious rebukes might be received with an innocent chuckle.

There are local differences – differences of speech forms, differences of relationships, that might involve different responses. What is 'excessive familiarity' in one school might be encouraged practice in another, deriving not necessarily from traditional/progressive forms of teaching, but traditional relationships in the area. The teacher new to an area quickly has to monitor the folk customs and idioms that have prevailed over the years, and match his strategies accordingly.

With these differences in mind, it would be possible to draw up a list of strong and weak control techniques that were situationally specific (i.e. appropriate to the immediate situation). Among the weak techniques would be:

(1) cultural, sexual, age or local misdirection, as discussed above;
(2) confused techniques such as authoritarian or role one moment, progressive or personal the next, so that 'you never know where you are with him';
(3) techniques that are applied without conviction, or which allow room for manoeuvre: 'Not *too* much talking please!' 'We never talk, sir!' 'Not too much noise please! As long as it's a working noise!'

Both of these last two cases suffer from the underlying rules not being clearly and firmly established; possibly in the teacher's own mind. A typical illustration is the teacher who talks and shouts too much – the more he shouts, the less he achieves, only adding to the general hubbub. Another example is the well-known 'insubstantial threat'. There are also:

(4) routinised techniques, the rationale for which has become lost, even to the teacher: 'We asked Mr. Hardcastle why not, and he said it was a school rule. So we asked him why it was a school rule, and he couldn't answer.'

(5) What we might call 'external fraternising' techniques, which involve appeals to loyalty to some external code based in adult, teacher rationale, such as 'being British', 'playing the game', 'owning up'; and appeals to reason, fairness, commonsense, thought for others. There is a mixture of liberal means in the 'appeal' and authoritarian rule, hence the weakness.

The best examples of this often occur during School Assembly: 'You may have been watching the World Cup lately and identifying with your football heroes. Listen to this story about Grace Darling, a hero of our time. (Reads, and embroiders, punching message home). As I looked round the sports field yesterday morning, I wondered how many would be able to say, like Grace Darling, "What would I do?", "What *could* I do?" . . . If you can never rise to the little challenges, you'll never be able to rise to the bigger ones. . . .' This is a clear example of the 'playing fields of Eton' ideology, with a token attempt to make it relevant through the boys' great interest in football. This latter, however, is totally crushed by the irrelevance to pupils of that particular ideology, which so prevails in our schools. I discuss this further below.

(6) Humiliating techniques, such as sarcasm, shouting and showing up. These may appear effective but they bully into submission, and like all such actions build up resentment and future deviance, and hence only compound disorder.

Stronger forms of control are:

(1) Cultural etc. identification (e.g. the 'lurid language' teacher with the deviant boys);

(2) Clear-cut techniques well signalled e.g. with an authoritarian style, clear rules, scrupulously observed, with undeviating language during 'lesson time'; or, conversely, with more libertarian styles, no recourse to authoritarianism (which could explode the common accord that might have been gained, raising doubts about the teacher's real intentions and his real relationship with them);

(3) techniques for which the underlying rationale is clearly visible; and

(4) internally consistent techniques.

However, these techniques are situationally specific, their aims are short-term, in the main, to achieve a localised control. Behind them lie more powerful forces than are contained in the immediate surround, forces that have their origin in society. This is not the place to discuss this connection in detail, though we might note one effect that is of particular interest concerning disciplinary forms in school. This is what has been termed 'cultural lag'.

The structure of society changes, but values and beliefs, ways of living, especially how one copes with the world, and other cultural forms which owe their origin to structural forces, lag behind.

This gap will be exaggerated by three further factors. One is the speed of social change: the faster the change, the more the lag and the greater the disjunction. The second is a generational one: younger people are obviously more adaptable. Coming to meet social forms for the first time they are more open to the possibilities, more outgoing, more amenable to change. Older people have made their adaptations, often quite painfully. They are not so easily shaken off or adjusted. The third is the conservative nature of institutions, and especially institutions like schools.

Lag affects schools in many ways. One is through tradition, which itself plays on memory and status and seeks to present a face of success through erstwhile symbols generated in a previous age in response to previous requirements. This possibly explains the persistence of Latin for the greater part of this century as a prime subject. Also the persistence of certain religious forms and assemblies. The injunction 'Now bow your heads, and let's say the Lord's Prayer' carries a wealth of symbolic meaning, not least in the spectacle of the bowed heads, a solid sheaf of brushed, tidy, glistening pupil hair. 'Holy' language, too, remains and is often delivered with much strength and flourish: 'Whatsoever your hand findeth to do, *do* it with all thy might!' was one upon which the boys at the back of the hall put a different construction from the Headmaster. Another example is the invention of 'instant tradition' by newly established secondary schools in the thirties.[5] The same applies to disciplinary forms – they live on, by tradition. But another 'lagging' force acts on these as well, namely their continued apparent success as disciplinary forms. There is no doubt that the standard teacher in our schools is faced with vast problems of order. It is no wonder that those that have proved efficacious in the past should maintain their currency.

All these factors bear on the young teacher entering schools today – the speed of change, tradition, his own biography, the influence of older teachers, the disciplinary problems together with having to cope with the kids' 'trying out' phase activities, his own instincts and desires, the lessons of teacher training – so that before long the would-be friendly fraterniser (the approach perhaps most prominently suggested by his instinctive response to those of his own generation in the current age) has doubts about his approach, and his language, and is soon telling them to 'shut up', 'keep quiet', 'get out', 'stand up straight', 'hands on heads', like his more experienced colleagues. These signals usually work. The kids are conditioned to respond to them. They can provide a blissful breathing space. But at the end of the day they are unsatisfactory, for they belong to a previous age. They may have situational effect, but they have societal irrelevance.

One aspect of the irrelevance is 'an overemphasis on material considerations, technology, economic indicators, massiveness of scale, impersonality of modes of functioning and other characteristics associated with the development of industrial society. Slater refers to this technologically dominated culture as the "old culture" and suggests that there are signs of a "new culture" emerging which stresses cooperation (instead of competition) sharing (instead of individualistic accumulation) and the cultivation of human happiness (rather than achievement).'[6] That does not occur, however, by chance, nor does it occur in a social vacuum.

One of the most pressing problems today is interrelationships in a multi-cultural society. We have a mixture of ethnic groups, social classes and sub-classes, religious groups, and generations (more, as people live longer). We can approach the job of teaching them in several ways, all highly charged politically. One is to attempt to impose a dominant culture upon them all, at least to get them to acknowledge a hierarchy of forms, so that their behaviour is conditioned to accept, even support, a class system of privilege. Some do this by choice, but many do this unintentionally, bending to the pressures of cultural lag and situational constraint.

Another is to acknowledge that within this diversity, and within the internal dynamics generated within these several cultures, lies a greater potential for social change towards cohesion rather than conflict. It would recognise, for example, class cultural forms as accommodations to circumstances, and seek to identify the sources of strength of these adaptations, rather than nullify them. It would recognise periodic experimentation among the young not as aberrations from the golden path, but as possibilities for change, as responses to current material circumstances in the world outside school, and as such, candidates for inclusion within the teacher's schema of realationships. Teddy boys, mods and rockers, greasers, hell's angels, hippies, punk rockers, football hooligans – all offer commentaries on the current state and structure of society. Those groups are of an extreme kind, but it would not be difficult to show that the rest of their generational cohorts, even the conformist ones, were not dissimilar in certain ways; and that these groups have, in fact, *forced* considerable changes in schools over the last twenty-five years. These changes could have been achieved with less difficulty with a more cohesive outlook, and certainly more needs to be achieved in the future.

In the mediation of these changes, language plays a particularly important part. It is our major means of communicating, and living together cohesively means communicating con-

structively. This does not mean the teacher imposing his forms
of speech or seeking to change or obliterate the pupils. Nor
does it necessarily mean joining them in their forms of speech.
It implies the cultivation of what I will call a 'discourse of the
middle ground', that is a form of communication to which all
contribute creatively. This is a public language not resembling
the commonly understood civil discourse which pervades
public life, and which is functionary, and depersonalised. On
the contrary, the 'discourse of the middle ground' is highly
personal, and because all contribute to it on an equal basis,
personal identification and creativity are encouraged.

What are its distinguishing features, this language of the
fraternal community? It is marked by mutual respect and
trust, a shared concern; a regard for individuals in their own
right, and as 'whole' persons; and for their several cultures
and life-plans; equivalent power bases; mutual interest and
concern – so that the effort to reach the middle ground comes
naturally and is felt to be worth making; recognition of the
need, on both sides, which facilitates the creation of opportunities for such discourse; an internalising and experiential
approach to knowledge and learning, and a 'growth' model of
morals and values. The distinctive tone of such discourse is
warm, open and friendly. There are fair shares for all in the
allocation of speaking time, general recognition of the
therapeutic qualities of talk, and the development of a neutral
vocabulary. This follows all the criteria specified above. For
example, one will not employ terms and idioms that one
knows will give offence to other parties to the conversation.
The teachers will not denigrate, ingratiate, patronise or moral-
ise, and the pupil – if he can do it without being inhibited, and
most of them can – will not employ, for example, the colourful
or parochial language he might use in interaction with his
peers or family, nor choose inappropriate topics of conversation with deliberate discomforting intent. For example,
appropriate subjects in the staffroom or playground are not
necessarily suited to the classroom. Overheard conversations
are frequently embarrassing because they offend personal
norms.

The mistake is to assume that such talk is indicative of basic
character, or 'wrong'. Even the teacher quoted previously who

thought one class of pupils 'revolting' illustrated his ability to make contact with 'an idle waster in class.' Meeting him as an individual, he reported 'I had a talk with him the other day – his background, family, what he's going to do – and for the first time I felt I was getting through to him'.

Some teachers do manage to accommodate to some degree or other, like this American teacher:

> These children, they look you straight in the eye when they use those words. I have never learned how to use these four-letter words until I came into contact with them. I never could even swear. Now I'm brazen. I had a fight with my husband one day. You know what I said to him? 'Fuck you.' (Laughs.) And I never talked that way. (Laughs.) I hear it all the time from the students. They use it the way we use 'eat' and 'talk.' They don't say 'pennies,' they say, 'f-pennies.' Every word. It's a very descriptive adjective. (S. Terkel, *Working*, Penguin, 1977 p. 407).

The middle ground is characterised by individuality. Because each individual contributes something, and because others' contributions are measured for him personally, he feels that he has a stake in it – it is his. As Barnes *et al* advise, 'The more teachers foster the initiative of their pupils the more likely it is that their pupils will develop a confidence in their own use of language. The less they attempt to verbalise ideas for their pupils the less stereotyped will their pupils' language be.'[7] This contrasts with standard classroom language, which almost of necessity, because of numbers, treats children as ciphers. Willis warns that 'disaffected working-class kids respond not so much to the style of individual teachers and the content of education, as to the structure of the school and the dominant teaching paradigm in the context of their overall class cultural experience and location.'[8] A reform of the school structure, a review of authoritarianism, and a recognition of the existence and validity of their own cultures would perhaps give the style of individual teachers and the content of education more of a chance. It follows that, if it is considered important, more opportunities should be devised to give the teacher more room for manoeuvre to cultivate middle ground discourse. This will then carry or sustain whatever 'classroom talk' is necessary, instead of being dominated by it. The imperatives will disappear, for the order is contained in the underlying middle ground, which could always be appealed to as the dominant mode.

The language of the middle ground is certainly *not* artificial (through which one might get accused of 'wetness', 'sucking up', 'creeping') nor authoritarian, and hence one-sided; nor is it indulgent or paternalistic; it is not based on the Protestant Ethic nor social Darwinism; it is not marked by power relationships, nor by confusion and bewilderment, fear and distrust. It is not underwritten by impositional models of morals and values, and external notions of knowledge. Nor, finally, is it Utopian, because it does happen, even in schools, with certain teachers, and there are several examples in the literature of the middle ground of discourse in various fields.[9] It is still very far, however, from becoming the predominant mode, which still remains the authoritarian/traditional model, often behind a progressive front.

It certainly is not easy to accomplish, let alone sustain, the use of this language, given the difficult circumstances most teachers work in, the history of teaching, and 'cultural lag'. One must have the freedom to make use of all the best elements of one's own speech patterns that are 'open' to the same unambiguous interpretations by others. In the use and re-use of all these various elements that go to the making of the discourse of the middle ground, one both learns and contributes to others' learning a language through which a multicultural society can interact in a meaningful, constructive and cooperative manner. It is directly opposed to the largely authoritarian past and to modes governed by class differences. It is the language of order for a communal future.

NOTES

[1] B. Bernstein, *Class, Codes and Control*, Vols 1 and 2, Routledge & Kegan Paul, 1973

[2] M. Stubbs, *Language, Schools and Classrooms*, Methuen, 1976, p. 83: See also, M. Stubbs, 'Keeping in touch: Some functions of teacher talk,' M. Stubbs and S. Delamont, (Eds), *Explorations in Classroom Observation*, Wiley, 1976

[3] See S. Delamont, *Interaction in the Classroom*, Methuen, 1976. Also, P. Atkinson and S. Delamont, 'Mock-ups and Cock-ups: The Stage Management of Guided Discovery Instruction', in P. Woods and M. Hammersley (Eds), *The Process of Schooling*, Routledge & Kegan Paul, 1976

[4] D. Barnes, J. Britton and H. Rosen, *Language, the Learner and the School*, Penguin, p. 55. See also S. Delamont[3]; P. Atkinson and S. Dela mont[3]; M. Hammersley, 'The Mobilisation of Pupil Attention'; P. Woods and M. Hammersley[3]

[5] See R. Bell and N. Grant, *A Mythology of British Education*, Panther, 1974

[6] R. Rapoport and R. N. Rapoport, *Leisure and the Family Life Cycle*, Routledge & Kegan Paul, p. 356

[7] D. Barnes *et al*[4], p. 167

[8] P. Willis, *Learning to Labour*, Saxon House, 1978, pp. 188-9

[9] See for example P. Willis[8]; P. Willis, *Profane Culture*, Routledge & Kegan Paul, 1978; H. J. Parker, *View from the Boys*, David & Charles, 1974; D. Robins and P. Cohen, *Knuckle Sandwich*, Penguin, 1978; S. Hall and T. Jefferson (Eds), *Resistance through Rituals*, Hutchinson, 1976; J. Patrick, *A Glasgow Gang Observed*, Eyre Methuen, 1973; P. Marsh, E. Rosser and R. Harre, *The Rules of Disorder*, Routledge & Kegan Paul, 1978; S. Terkel, *Working*, Penguin, 1977

8

Richard Martin and Jenifer Smith, whose contribution comes next, both teach at Countesthorpe College. I am never sure how much to explain about Countesthorpe, for in some circles it is a household word. However, many of those who claim to know all about it turn out to have sketchy or mistaken ideas, so some basic explanation is called for.

Countesthorpe is a Leicestershire upper school, which is to say that it is a comprehensive school for pupils of fourteen to eighteen years of age. What marks it out particularly is that right from the start it has been run on lines sufficiently different from most state schools for it to be justly labelled 'progressive' or 'radical'. It lays claim to be democratic, on the grounds that all decisions are corporately made — the head really is that primus inter pares *which so many others claim to be. There is no obvious hierarchical structure — no heads of department for example. Instead, teaching is done by 'teams' of the kind described in Richard and Jenifer's chapter. There is as little coercion of children as possible, on the grounds that a child forced into learning is not going to learn anyway. Thus, relationships between teacher and taught are informal and easy — the aim is that learning should be collaborative rather than didactic. All the other, headline making features — Christian names, common loos — stem from, and are a natural part of, a coherent fundamental approach to the nature of learning.*

Not surprisingly, this is a setting where the twin concepts of 'discipline' and 'punishment' are not easy to separate out from everything else that goes on. This is partly because the teachers are more relaxed about their pupils than teachers in more authoritarian establishments tend to be, so that an action which might be treated as a prelude to mass insurrection at one school will hardly raise an eyebrow at Countesthorpe. Mainly, though, it is because at Countesthorpe teachers and pupils are partners in learning, and it is not all that appropriate for some arbitrary level of 'control' to be striven for.

Richard and Jenifer, therefore, have written about their work within the 'team'. They have fixed upon two examples of pupils who were potentially disruptive and have shown how the flexibility of approach which is possible at Countesthorpe was used to avoid any sort of ultimate head-on clash between an unwilling pupil and an immoveable authority.

A Case for Conversation: Teams at Countesthorpe

RICHARD MARTIN AND JENIFER SMITH

Adults and children, like adults with each other, can associate well only in worthy interests and pursuits, only through a community of subject matter and engagement which extends *beyond* the circle of their intimacy.
'I, Thou and It' from *The Informed Vision* by David Hawkins.[1]

What we hope to do in this chapter is to describe an opportunity. It is an opportunity afforded us in our teaching to 'associate well' with students, not just by knowing them, but also, as the quotation suggests, by engaging with them in their learning, in a collaborative effort which can be mutually exciting and rewarding. Such a view of learning provides the framework for considerations of discipline: behaviour problems and learning difficulties can become part and parcel of the relationship between teacher and student, rather than extraneous distractions which interfere with an already established curriculum. It is our experience that education must be fitted to the student, adapted to his particular needs and interests; learning, and the problems which accompany it, need to be made part of a continuing conversation between teacher and student. The opportunity we try to describe, then, is not one which merely eases the traditional relationship between teacher and student, but one which substantially alters the focus of that relationship, encouraging the student to direct and control the course of his own learning. It is learning, therefore, which is at the centre of the relationship and provides the framework for 'associating well'.

What follows is a description of a possible context for such a view of learning – the team system which has been developing at Countesthorpe College over the last seven to eight years, and in which we have both been involved for a good deal of that time. We also include examples of two students' work in the hope that these will help define our approach more clearly, and show some of the ways in which we have attempted to explore and take advantage of our opportunity so far.

Teams, it should be said at the outset, do not involve the notion of team-teaching as often conceived; rather they are mini-schools within a much larger school. They offer students the chance to exercise autonomy in choosing what they learn and how they learn it over a wide area of the curriculum, with the help and guidance of teachers to whom they are well known. The aim of encouraging autonomy was to some extent thwarted in the early years of the school under a system which prescribed a compulsory 'core' of subjects for part of the week, and allowed 'options' at others; the contradiction inherent in such an arrangement was further compounded by a fairly rigid separation of subject areas which precluded many kinds of choices, and a familiar pattern of pastoral organisation which meant that students were rarely taught by their tutors for more than a few lessons a week.[2]

The team system, then, places at its centre the tutor, in both his pastoral and his academic roles, as one who works along-side the student, pursuing interests and enthusiasms not necessarily his own, which may take him beyond the limits of his own subject specialism. Thus, subjects taught in a team vary according to the teachers who comprise that team, but normally cover English, Maths and the general area of the Humanities. The tutor also has an important responsibility to help his students achieve a balanced timetable: the school offers students choice over the whole curriculum, and subjects taught outside team vary again, but normally include those subjects which need specialist equipment or a specialist area, such as Art and Craft, Design, Physics, Typing and Physical Education. A student's participation in any of these subjects will often entail a difference in emphasis, and he will go to that area at a prescribed time for the purpose of that particular activity. The specialist teacher can offer expertise the tutor may lack; the tutor offers support to the student in his choices, and helps him make sense of his learning over the whole range of his activities. In recent years, more subjects have been incorporated into teams in different ways: art teachers have come into teams at certain times of the week to encourage greater participation; some teams are developing fully equipped science laboratories, with resident specialists for part of the week. This has offered many advantages: it has helped blur distinctions between 'team' and 'specialist' subjects; it allows students the chance to pursue their particular enthusiasms in new ways over a wider area of the curriculum; it allows tutors to be more involved in a wider area of their students' learning; and it offers specialist teachers the opportunity to work more closely with both student and tutor, and to be better informed about the whole course of a student's learning.

Since teams differ in certain aspects of composition and organisation, let us take as a model the team we work in. Our physical base comprises a suite of rooms grouped round a central open area. This operates throughout the week as both a working and a social base for our 130 students who stay with us during the fourth and fifth years of their secondary schooling. Six tutors have their bases here, and work with their students for about ten periods out of a twenty-period week. Tutor groups usually number about twenty-five, though this will often vary according to the experience of the tutor or his commitments outside the team; they are of mixed ability, and are usually built around existing friendship groups. One of the tutors is a specialist Maths teacher who in addition to his own tutorial responsibilities (he has a rather smaller group) teaches Maths, often with the assistance and involvement of the tutors. We have also established over the years in our area a photographic darkroom, and a room equipped for tape-recording which also serves as a withdrawal room for careers interviews, or any of those occasions when greater privacy is required. We also have a science laboratory. This is run by a specialist Science teacher, and students are usually timetabled initially under the general heading of Science, though this will usually develop later into the more specific areas of Biology, Chemistry or General Science. Our scientist is with us for about half the week, and although Science is a comparatively

recent addition to our team, it has already offered many new
possibilities.

For us as tutors, then, our primary responsibility is not just
to be concerned with the general well-being of our students in
minutes snatched during registration, but to be involved with
them in their learning in whatever directions that learning
takes, as far as we are able. We may have to call on other team
tutors, or go outside the team to specialists, but on the whole
we spend about half the week with a tutor group whose
activities and interests are as diverse as we can cope with.
Rarely does it happen that one student will be engaged in the
same work as others, though group activities can and do
occur. As it happens, we are both English specialists by training – and we teach English in the sixth form – but our students' work takes us far beyond the confines of that specialism;
we have been happy that this should be so and believe it is
vital if we are to encourage the kind of learning which will
engage and excite our students, and allow them to pursue
their enthusiasms rigorously and strenuously. If the idea of
doing without an established curriculum sounds alarming, it
should be remembered that each lesson does not begin in
chaos and continue in anarchy: for each student in each lesson
there is a context, and work is seen as a continuum. There will
be a hiatus when interest is lost or work completed, when new
work needs to be initiated or ideas offered which will stimulate
a new, even short-lived interest, but team allows time for conversation. It is through the continuing conversation between
teacher and student that much of the learning advances; and
conversation provides a metaphor for the manner in which the
relationship is conducted: relaxed, informal, concerned. In
this way all the problems which urge themselves upon the
tutor, many of which might otherwise pose themselves as disciplinary problems, as interruptions or distractions from the
real business of education, are allowed to become part of the
conversation.

To illustrate the point further, we will cite some examples of
the kinds of work we have been engaged in with two of our
students, which we hope will go some way to clarify our
approach. As seems appropriate in this context, they are students who have presented each of us with particular problems

in terms of behaviour or learning difficulties. The first example sketches, briefly of necessity, the work done by one student with one of us, Richard Martin, over the course of his fourth year. It aims to show the way in which one student's interest in a particular area broadened and developed over the course of a year.

John arrived with a reputation for being somewhat disruptive. In his past, he had been described as lazy and of very limited ability. He had a reading age of about seven years and some quite severe learning problems, and I viewed his joining my group with some trepidation, and I confess, with little enthusiasm. At our initial meeting, before he joined the school, he seemed taciturn and nervous, unlike the group of friends who accompanied him, who seemed relaxed and enthusiastic about the prospect of coming to a new school. I determined over the holiday that I would try to engage him from the beginning as far as possible in activities that would not require much reading or writing, at least for a while.

Our starting point was photography. John talked to me a little about the farm in the village where he lives, some three miles from the school, and about the amount of spare time he spent on the farm. I suggested he take a camera home with him one night in order to record anything he cared to of the farm and his work there. He did not return the next day. I was, not surprisingly, annoyed both with him, for taking advantage of me, as I saw it, and with myself for having encouraged, even authorised apparently, a day off, with camera, and all within the first few days of the school year. On the following day he returned, with the camera mercifully, and a roll of used film. He had, he explained, waited all day for a calf that was due to be born, and which had not made its appearance until the evening. We developed the negatives together, and then I printed them, explaining to John very sketchily the process involved. The photographs were a considerable success, both in terms of their quality – though the calf was a little murky in the twilight – and of the record they provided him with of events he recalled time and again for himself and his friends.

From these photographs sprang, in the first place, a tape

recording which I transcribed for him, describing each picture in some detail, and later, a series of drawings and paintings produced over a period of weeks, of a tractor. These tractor paintings, based on his own photograph, involved painstaking effort, for John wished for a precise and meticulous representation. There were many versions: some were abandoned early on, others would be near completion when with a shout of frustration they would end in the bin. John would assert that they were not up to his standard – and indeed, one could see why when he at last completed a painting to his satisfaction.

This obsession with detail and with achieving a self-imposed and very exacting standard came to characterise much of John's work, and threw new light on someone of whom I had previously had very limited expectations. There were other paintings at this period, many of them patterns, and one – a country scene in snow viewed through a window frame, the glass frosted outside – was very sophisticated and particularly fine, and quite unlike the tractor paintings of which he was most proud. Also around this time, John began an elaborate map of the farm, starting with a crude sketch map done from memory, and developing into a big map enlarged from smaller Ordnance Survey maps. This too required painstaking effort and he would spend whole mornings or afternoons on it, often with very little help from me, and I was frequently on tenterhooks that this too would end in the bin. It did not, and he was rightly pleased with the finished product.

In the course of some historical work being done by another boy in the team of the same area, we were presented with a map produced in 1888 for the purposes of a sale of the farm, together with a handbill. This gave rise to the discovery of a former fulling mill on the farm. John had insisted on occasions that the stream which flows through the farm must have taken a different course at some time for there was, he said, a dried-up stream bed to be seen which directly by-passed the meandering course of the stream. The process of research which ensued was lengthy and too complicated to recount here, but it became increasingly obvious from our studies of maps, directories and local histories that there had been a mill in that area, though it had ceased functioning by the end of the eighteenth century, and that this dried-up and overgrown bed could well have been the former leet of the mill. The 1888 map did much to confirm this, with its reference to a 'Fulling Mill Close'.

The day John took me to visit the site was a very exciting one, and he, normally reserved, even terse, rarely volunteering more than I asked for, was most articulate. He explained to me where the leet must have been, where he thought the mill would have been sited, and where the millpond probably was. He had thought it through most carefully, and I was therefore all the more dismayed to find that the stream ran in the other direction from what I had expected – I don't know why – and that a six-foot bank now barred the stream from flowing through John's 'leet'. He waded through the stream in his shoes, in excitement and bravado. He had the answer, and found the words to express his thesis: 'Assume,' he said, 'that the leet had been filled in to make it useful for farming land, and assume that the stream has cut a deeper bed to cope with the extra water. . . .' Subsequent research has not proved his theory, but the evidence, culled from numerous sources, is strong.

We have not since had such excitement in our learning, and to some extent, what has followed has not engaged John so fully, though it has provided him with ample material for many written accounts, each one carefully written and rewritten with characteristic effort, with more photography – he is now a competent photographer able to print and develop pictures of good quality – with more map work, drawings and imagined reconstructions of a working mill. He has a bulging folder to show for his work of which he is justly proud. What I have described here is the mainstream of work that occupied us in team lessons for about a year. Elsewhere, John has pursued his enthusiasm for tractors and machines in Vehicle Engineering, has attended remedial reading lessons regularly, and spent a good deal of time in the design area. He has also attended Maths lessons, though with less enthusiasm, and certainly has not since matched the afternoon when he worked for over two and a half hours, including break, adding up the acreage of the farm on a calculator.

My example here is, perhaps, a dramatic one, for John has had on occasion some spectacular successes, and there is a unity about the development of his work which may not be entirely typical, but he does serve to illustrate a further quotation from David Hawkins, whom we quoted at the beginning of the chapter: '. . . the first act in teaching, the first goal, necessary to all others, is to encourage . . . engrossment. Then the child comes alive for the teacher as well as the teacher for the child. They have a common theme for discussion, they are involved together in the world.'

What I would wish to stress about the work I have described very sketchily is the mutual interest and excitement we shared in the process of discovery; neither of us was master of the subject, and indeed it was often the student who pushed ahead where I was reluctant or sceptical, and John showed extraordinary determination and perseverance. His work also, perhaps, serves to demonstrate some of the dangers involved for us as teachers in our expectations and labelling of children's behaviour and abilities. I expected him to present me with many behaviour problems: this has not been so, and we have developed a working relationship which has stayed us through some bleak patches when work was slow, and supplied a framework in which to be 'involved together in the world'. John still has many frustrations, and is occasionally given to outbreaks of temper; he remains taciturn on the whole, and his attitude to me is ironical, often mock-aggressive. On the other hand, he derives much satisfaction from his school work, and is relaxed with his teachers.

More importantly, he has revealed abilities and qualities quite beyond what I had expected. To do this, I have had to adapt to his particular mode of learning: he does not like much help, but prefers to feel in command of his work, and I have been of most direct use in providing material when I felt he was ready for it. He works obsessively in bursts of intense activity, often involving long periods of concentration; he likes to work at one task at a time, often engaging in an activity or pursuit over a period of weeks. For my part, I have often done little more than watch, afraid that the spell his work seemed to cast on him would be broken; I noted early on in my records, 'He is very tolerant of the barren patches between each new burst. I seem, willy-nilly, to be doing it right with him – I think.' It felt like that, and there was sometimes a sense of strain in not intervening, but it has been his engrossment, nurtured and fostered, that has allowed him to take charge of his learning. It is his engrossment that has stayed him for over a year, and has provided him with work in history and archaeology, in art, photography and map making, as well as helping him develop his skills in reading and writing. He has engaged in material apparently far beyond his limited reading ability. He has mastered skills that have stretched him and has displayed a fiercely intellectual interest quite outside my limited expectations. He has also, I hope, gained in self-esteem and been 'involved in the world'.

Unlike John, the student that Jenifer Smith has chosen to write about, Simon, presented himself to her in such a way as openly to challenge her to recognise him as he was, and to set about solving various problems with him.

When Simon first arrived in my group he was in some ways rather a loner. He seemed a bright, lively boy with a wide range of interests and a lot of curiosity; I had been rather looking forward to teaching him since the interesting conversation I had had with him in the high school. I knew that he had a relatively low reading age and soon discovered that although he did not lack ideas, he rarely wrote more than a couple of sentences at a time. My first term, as far as Simon was concerned, was one of worry and frustration. He would not sit in one place for long, he hid away scrappy bits of writing he had started, he left work at home. We tried all sorts of subjects and ideas without success, and now and again Simon would say, in that tone of voice which absolved him of all responsibility, 'Just set me something and I'll do it.' As I pointed out to him at the time, I had set him any number of things to do which he had not even begun to complete.

At the end of the Christmas term a girl in my group took some photographs of her work in a crèche and, since Simon and his friend Mick were interested, I showed them how to print photographs. Once in the darkroom, Simon was really annoying and both Mick and I became very irritated by him.

If Mick was making a print, Simon fooled about with the timer, saying that he had started it going when he had not, or not telling Mick that the correct time was up until too late. In the end I was really angry with him, he had been very inconsiderate, stupidly thoughtless. I was glad that at least Mick had grasped the basic ideas involved in printing and had enjoyed doing it, despite Simon.

It was really for Mick's sake that I allowed Simon to continue working on photography, although I could see that Simon too was excited by this work, and I hoped that Mick's serious and sensible approach would have a somewhat sobering effect on his friend. At the beginning of the Spring term I recorded in my teaching diary:

> The nicest thing that has happened today is that Simon and Mick spent the afternoon in the darkroom and have produced some splendid prints, some good solarisation and a strange double exposure – a tiny head inside a face, which makes the whole thing look like some kind of beast. It's really exciting when they do things like this, and although I was happy for Mick to go into the darkroom on his own, I was worried about the potentially explosive presence of Simon. Anyway, he's making a real success of this and he shows it!

This was the turning point for Simon. He began to take his own photographs and to print them on his own. He was sought after by other students who also wished to learn how to print photographs. For a while we were without an enlarger, during which time we made pinhole cameras; Simon worked on this with a rather academic girl, in many ways a rather unlikely partner. Not only was he able to guide her through much of their work together, but also saw far more possibilities for the pinhole camera than she appeared to. Helen proved to be important in Simon's development: she took him seriously, respected him and at the same time set about the work in a calm, conscientious fashion – a good foil to his more ebullient approach.

Since that time, most of Simon's work has sprung from his interest in photography. He has made photogenic paper according to Fox Talbot's early formula, has experimented with negative reversal techniques for use with pinhole photography, and has taken a great interest in the photography of others. Recently, he has engaged in the problem of recording the swing of a pendulum with light on photographic paper. His first attempts were unsatisfactory and from then on he worked away at the problem in a way that was typical of him. He rarely seemed to let it out of his mind, tenaciously pursuing his aim and overcoming obstacles in his way. In his first attempts he managed only to record the light as it fell nearest the paper. He used a small light bulb, first painted to leave only a pin prick of light, and later encased in a plastic film holder. Neither of these methods was satisfactory and he continued to consider the problem of the light while fixing up a pendulum which swung to make an interesting pattern. But how was he to know what kind of pattern the pendulum was making? At this stage he worked mostly with our science teacher. First he tried ink, but the flow was not fine enough and ran too fast. He then tried sand, but the grains jumped around the paper so that you could not see the pattern at all. At this point, the problem of simply recording the pattern of a pendulum swing had taken over Simon's initial problem, but he still kept returning to the problem of the light. His experiments attracted much comment and helpful advice and somehow he got around to the idea of using something like golden syrup which, as he said, once it had started to flow, would draw itself out of the swinging container. This led to him using Marvin Medium to record the pattern which he then covered with sand in order to preserve it. I found the patterns very pleasing in themselves, but Simon, having made a satisfactory pendulum with a suitable arrangement of weights, was more concerned to return to the original task. A teacher passing the pendulum at work had suggested that fibre optics might be the answer and we were lucky enough to obtain a small length of this from the physics teacher. Simon was rather sceptical at this stage but fixed up the pendulum and the fibre optic in the darkroom. He ensured there was no light spillage and tried once again to record the pendulum swing on photographic paper. It worked. I was delighted. Simon was pleased, but because the paper was quite small, the patterns were rather jerky. He had seen plans while at work on his pendulum for a harmonograph. He is now in the process of making one and is determined to set it up in the darkroom.

He has developed a way of working that is uniquely Simon. When he has a problem to solve – and this is when he seems happiest – his mind works away at it all the time. He will walk about, look at his equipment, follow me or the science teacher about, posing questions, postulating solutions, requiring the attention of interested adults at various crucial points, needing to share his ideas, pessimism, success. Other students find his work interesting and ask about it, though few show such a strong drive to solve problems.

When I first began to work with Simon, he seemed to have few close friends, and I found his childish behaviour frustrating and annoying; he would nag and mither me until I could stand it no longer. At about the same time as his first work in photography he asked me if I ever got tired of him. I told him that I did get fed up when he was so childish, and his face fell. I thought at the time that I say things to my students that I would never say to my contemporaries, and yet, in a way, Simon forced me to face that particular issue with him. For him, our facing some of his personal problems together was important and as much a part of finding a way to work as anything else we did. One of his problems was that he could not settle to work and my chief concern was that he should not only settle but become thoroughly involved in some aspect of learning. It seems to me now that those two aims were inextricable, and that a sense of involvement and excitement in learning and in developing ideas is essential in helping the student to develop and to recognise himself as a person; and that a sense of self as a growing, maturing individual, worthy of respect and respecting others as such, is equally important in the way it encourages involvement and an excitement about learning.

It seems that the way we work in team constantly gives rise to unusual opportunities both for the individual and for groups of people. It allows for an exchange of ideas and feelings, not only at an academic level, but also at a social and a more personal level, which arises from and fosters a growing self-

knowledge and an awareness of others. Jenifer Smith here
records a conversation with some of her students to illustrate
the point.

On one afternoon, I was sitting at a large table with a number
of students. Simon was looking at some suggestions for writing
an autobiography. He asked suddenly, 'How can I write down
what sort of person I am? I don't know. What sort of person
am I?' I agreed that it was difficult to write about oneself in
that way, and others began to join the conversation. I think I
said that other people do tend to see you differently from the
way you see yourself, and Simon really pushed me to say what
sort of person I thought he was. I made a few suggestions and
we got on to talking more generally about what sort of people
we are. The students were keen to know how I saw them,
which I handled as honestly as I felt was possible – which is
not to say I lied, but I did leave some things unsaid. Everyone
agreed that Diane would give as good as she got if a teacher
shouted at her, whereas Susan agreed that she was likely to 'go
mardy'. Susan talked quite a lot about herself, more than I
had ever known her to, saying that she did not like not to
please people, or to feel she was not liked, and that that feeling
or any reprimand would make her cross and upset. She was
quite strongly criticised by Simon, first for not being able to
take a joke, and then for always bringing her family into everything. Diane defended Susan in an outraged fashion and I,
feeling that a positive note was needed, talked about family
and friends being important to Susan, and said that she was
able to talk about them in an honest, thoughtful way – a way
in which Simon never would.

There was a pause for breath in which Simon took the
opportunity to say my problem was that I was always picking
on people, that teachers always picked on people. There were
general murmurs of agreement. I tried to say that you tried
hard not to, though it very often seemed that way. Were they
thinking of Paul, I asked? I was right. He is one of a group of
very noisy boys who I often have to ask to be quiet. Even if I
ask the group as a whole, it is Paul who jumps loudly to his
own defence. I mentioned this, that perhaps some people were
less tolerant of rebuke than others, that I myself hate to be told

I am in the wrong, though I am more likely to get upset like Susan than shout like Paul.

It was at this point we began to talk about how differently people react to the same thing. Ann said I did not have a sense of humour and explained that she thought this because I do not laugh at her jokes. I agreed, but pointed out that I find Simon's drier wit more to my taste. This brought Simon back to Susan's lack of any sense of humour. She replied that he was wrong, she need not necessarily find him funny, though she admitted she did not like the kind of teasing Simon gives her. Diane and Simon thought she was spoilt. Yes, she thought she was rather, but thought she was getting on better socially. We discussed and speculated more than it is useful to record here, but the feeling of the whole discussion was positive and friendly. Only that combination of people at that time could have said those things to each other.

My only worry at the time, and on reflection, had been Susan, who takes herself very seriously and, as she had confessed, is very much affected by the opinions of others. Two days later she gave me the next part of her autobiography to read. I am not sure if it was written after that conversation, but it was the most self-aware piece of writing that Susan had done. It mentioned her contacts with students in another tutor group which had given her much greater confidence, not only with girls but with a more mature group of boys than I have in my own group. I told Susan how much I thought she had changed; that she seemed much more self-assured, less worried, and I made some reference to the conversation we had had. I was reassured that she had, far from being upset by it, found it interesting. She had taken it all in her stride in a way which she would not have imagined herself doing a year before.

Team allows time and space for such personal speculation as this. Such conversations do occur and have their place, and are an important aspect of education that is often ignored or paid mere lip-service. Not, however, that all our students expect or want to engage in such considerations. John and Simon have presented themselves to us in entirely different ways; to some extent, John lacks the personal vocabulary to conduct such a conversation, but he also chooses to maintain a rather more formal and distant relationship with his tutor. It is important to remember in our informal way of working what it is proper for the student to retain of himself quite outside the teacher-student relationship; while some students make personal demands of their tutors, many others do not. We are not concerned to form special relationships, though we are often entrusted by our students with particular kinds of knowledge and understanding; rather we try to form durable, working relationships based on mutual respect.

Much respect is involved in the pursuit of learning. In engaging with our students in 'worthy interests and pursuits', respect for what is learnt can emerge naturally. In the act of 'associating well' through those pursuits, mutual respect between teacher and student can also be established. In our situation there are no formal sanctions, and our students are allowed many freedoms that would be considered inappropriate elsewhere; those freedoms, far from being merely permissive, are necessary to the learning we encourage our students to engage in. They are the necessary conditions for genuine enquiry and an open mind. That those freedoms are not often abused is thus a signal of the respect that we hope and believe learning can engender.

In no sense is what we advocate a panacea. Our necessarily brief accounts of students' work tend to be bland, since they not only give little sense of the excitement, but also leave out many of the frustrations involved. Working with students in the way we describe makes its own demands and brings its own problems; but the point that we would want to emphasise is that these are problems capable of solution for the most part, and without recourse to heavy-handed methods. In one sense, working closely with students creates its own kind of tolerance; knowing students well and engaging with them not only reduces anxiety and tension in the classroom, it actively promotes relaxed and congenial working conditions. Knowing through doing, through learning, creates that 'common theme for discussion', a way to be 'involved together in the world', and has its own dynamism: much is given, much taken, much shared by both teacher and student.

The team system we have described is in essence very simple, for it removes so many of the artificial and unnecessary obstacles and constraints to 'associating well', and replaces them with a continuing conversation between teacher and student, which affords both the opportunity for engrossment. Learning and all the obstacles to it are part of the conversation which is the essence of team. Team allows the teacher to become engrossed in his teaching as we hope it allows our students to become engrossed in learning. We hope it allows them room enough in which to be and grow and learn.

NOTES

[1] *The Informed Vision* by David Hawkins, Agathon Press. See particularly the chapter entitled 'I, Thou and It'.

[2] For a more detailed account of the development of the team system, see *The Countesthorpe Experience*, ed. John Watts, Unwin Education Books, especially the chapter *Schools within Schools* by Michael Armstrong and Lesley King.

9

'Psychology' is for many of us a vague term despite, or perhaps even because of, the exposure which we had to the subject at college or later in-service courses. Some teachers, indeed, are suspicious of it and regard educational psychologists, in particular, as people whose role is both indeterminate and hardly justified. This is part of the unfortunate tendency on the part of many teachers to act as if the only person who really knows what educational life is all about is the classroom teacher.

What every teacher needs to remember, I think, is that every time he makes a judgment about a child's work or behaviour, and bases future actions upon it, he is involved in psychology. In my own chapter I discussed rewards and punishments, and hinted at the possibility of there being a much more scientific approach to the subject. If we believe that children are affected by punishment or by rewards, and if we feel that the proper use of such devices might help us in dealing with difficult children, then we had better listen to the people who can tell us how to approach the subject systematically.

Ron Fawcett is interested in behaviour modification. The term is off-putting to some people, because it smacks of manipulation and seems to have little to do with education. But then, as I have said elsewhere, neither has punishment much to do with education, and yet we do it all the time. The teacher with a disruptive child wants strategies which work, so that he can get on with the job for which he is being paid. Without any doubt, he will be helped by what Ron Fawcett has to say.

The key to Ron Fawcett's approach, it seems to me, is its systematic nature. Many teachers do the things which he writes about – rewarding, giving attention, removing children from the classroom. How many, though, do them systematically, as the result of preliminary detailed observation, attending to one aspect of behaviour at a time?

Behaviour Modification in the Classroom

RON FAWCETT

Introduction

Behaviour modification is a systematic approach to the control of human behaviour. Its basic premise is that *behaviour is a function of its consequences*. Put more simply, this means that children behave in direct relation to the sorts of consequences which their behaviour has for them. Behaviour will be maintained if the pupil views the consequences as favourable and will tend to be discontinued if he views the consequences as unfavourable.

Certainly in research studies, behaviour modification implies an organised and regulated system of data collection and the keeping of precise records of behaviour and behaviour changes. This is of course the best way of determining whether particular types of intervention are producing desired effects. Measures are taken of the intensity and frequency of particular types of behaviour and consistent methods are used to regulate that behaviour. In schools it is sometimes difficult to be quite so systematic, but the more systematic one can be, the easier it will be to demonstrate that particular consequences follow particular interventions. It is also likely that the more consistent and systematic the treatment, the more effective it will prove to be.

Behaviour modification implies that the person who is carrying out the programme knows what is best for the subject being dealt with, and therefore assumes the right to institute certain procedures to try to modify the subject's behaviour. Behaviour modification techniques are therefore commonly used where certain persons are responsible for others and they have particular relevance for teachers in school and for parents inside and outside the home. This implied right to control the behaviour of others is sometimes questioned by critics of behaviour modification techniques. Other critics have pointed out that such techniques are essentially specific in nature, and do not take into account the 'whole' child. There is general agreement, however, that such techniques have some usefulness, and are particularly effective with young, hyperactive and backward children. To be effective at all, however, the techniques need to be carried out systematically and consistently.

Behaviour modification techniques depend essentially upon a careful analysis of the situation that is to be changed. Thus it is not very useful when introducing such an approach to start with the premise that a particular child is naughty or a pest or even disruptive. All these terms are too vague, and the actual behaviour of the child needs to be delineated far more carefully and accurately than this if the techniques are to be carried out effectively. One has to talk about specific behaviour, such as shouting out in the classroom, tearing up other children's work or being violent and attacking other children. It should be pointed out that the word 'behaviour' in psychological parlance means far more than conduct as such. As the psychologist views it, any actions carried out by people are viewed as behaviour in a general sense, and therefore, when behaviour modification techniques are brought to bear, they are not always specifically related to conduct. For instance, one could use behaviour modification techniques to try to deal with stammering, facial tics, smoking, or even watching too much television.

The systematic analysis of the behaviour of the child or adolescent usually includes measurements of frequency of particular behaviour, and also if possible its intensity. The behaviour should be described as objectively as possible – not only that of the subject but also that of some others in the same environment, such as the teacher or other pupils. Any person whose behaviour infringes directly on that of the child under scrutiny should be observed as well. This observation stage in analysing the situations in which behaviour modification is to be applied is a crucial part of the general procedure. The actual mapping of the behaviour and the responses induced by it may take a week or more. The initial observation stage is to enable the behaviour modifier to set up certain base lines to show clearly what kind of behaviour has to be modified, and the further essential purpose is to enable the modifier to generate ideas about what kinds of modification techniques are likely to be effective. Thus, at the end of a week's observation, it might be determined that a particular child attacked other children violently seventeen times, with an average occurrence of three to four times a day and with an apparently random incidence. One might also devise some sort of measure of the intensity of the particular attacks, although this might be unnecessary and in any case it would be too time-consuming. Once the frequency of behaviour – and possibly its intensity – has been determined in the initial stage, the behaviour modifier will from subsequent observations be able to determine whether or not his intervention techniques are bringing about improvement. He will make this assessment not purely subjectively in most cases, but will have objective information about frequency and possibly about intensity to guide him.

The initial observation stage may be carried out by the teacher himself (or herself) acting as his own observer and recording his own behaviour as well as that of the child and other children, or alternatively a classroom helper or another teacher may be called in to observe perhaps for half an hour at a time over five consecutive days. The extent of the initial observation period depends upon the availability of time and observers and also upon the general needs of the situation.

It is usually advisable when attempting to modify behaviour not to concentrate upon too wide a range of problems. Thus if a child is violent, has tantrums, swears, etc., it is often advisable to concentrate on one particular form of behaviour at a time, and perhaps decide to eradicate, say, the violence first, or the swearing, or whatever. Concentrating on several items of behaviour at once is likely to cause difficulty from various points of view, not least because the effectiveness of treatment is likely to be diluted, though one should certainly bear in mind the general principle that behaviour of any kind that is not rewarded is likely to disappear.

The principle of treatment is basically the psychological one of *reinforcement*. Reinforcement is rather similar to the popular concept of reward, but reinforcement can be negative as well as positive. Thus one may attempt to stamp out difficult behaviour, for instance, either by rewarding good behaviour or by offering some kind of unpleasant consequence for bad behaviour, or possibly by adopting both techniques. Broadly this is a conventional approach to the treatment of behaviour, but in fact conventional approaches are usually unsystematic, inconsistent, not closely controlled, and not closely mapped out. One of the major reasons why conventional approaches to child treatment frequently fail is that there is a lack of system and consistency in the approaches adopted, and there is often a mixture of different sorts of approach all used at the same time. They fail to work when the link between behaviour and treatment remains tenuous because of the different forms of treatment used.

There are many forms of negative and positive reinforcement, and to a very large extent the ones used will depend upon the personality of the particular child, his own motivations and needs, the personality of the teacher, and the kinds of resources available to the teacher or parent. (There is no reason incidentally why parents should not be brought in to cooperate in any behaviour programme adopted for a particular child – indeed the treatment may be enhanced by cooperation on the part of parents and by continuation at home at the end of the school day.) One might use consumable rewards such as sweets, especially with young children; one might use periods of time available or not available for watching television; one might use house points or money from parents or deprivation of treats in school or at home – or indeed sheer withdrawal of attention in some cases. The field of reinforcement is wide and there are many different approaches. With a particular child one might have to give an extended trial to two or three approaches before finding a successful one.

With many children the *attention* of an adult is extremely reinforcing, and many problems can be resolved merely by withdrawing attention and making no fuss at all about naughty behaviour. Conversely, one would pay attention to the child when he is behaving well. The general principle of attention or its withdrawal is frequently used to modify difficult and attention-seeking behaviour. Some forms of

hyperactive behaviour in children, however, are not suscept-
ible to such an approach, because the hyperactivity stems
from some neurological cause rather than from some
psychological need to be noticed. In such cases the behaviour
modification approach is likely to be other than the mere
withdrawal of attention.

Once one has dealt with the first item of difficult behaviour
and *extinguished* it (to use the technical term), one may proceed
to the modification of other forms of behaviour. It is commonly noticed, however, that once a particular behaviour has
been dealt with initially, there is often a commensurate
improvement in other difficult behaviour at the same time. It
is as though the extinction of one or two problems produces
consequences over a wider field, and erects a kind of scaffolding for the child's behaviour generally to be modified.

Dealing with classroom problems directly

It is becoming increasingly clear that teachers are looking for
a means of dealing with classroom problems directly. More
and more they are asking what they themselves can do within
their own classrooms to tackle directly certain behaviour problems with which they are faced. Behaviour modification gives
them a means of doing this, and a systematic set of skills to use
for the purpose. Behaviour modification stems directly from
psychology, but its main root is the study of normal, not
abnormal behaviour. It looks upon behaviour problems as
being related to learning, and not to psychological abnormal-
ity. It follows from this that more acceptable behaviour patterns can be learned if conditions are created that bring about
the more appropriate learning.

It also follows that the problems can be directly observed
and analysed in their own settings. If a child is a problem in
the classroom, he can be observed and treated in the classroom. There is no reason at all why teachers should not
become quite expert in behaviour modification, and should
not tackle a good many of their own problems directly. The
basic principles are as follows.

Behaviour is dependent upon its consequences If unacceptable
behaviour is followed by undesirable consequences, then that
behaviour will cease. The consequences must follow in a sys-

tematic and consistent way if the behaviour is to be modified effectively.

Control of contingencies This sounds a highly technical phrase, but it merely means that particular consequences are contingent upon particular sorts of behaviour. The modifier effectively controls the consequences of the child's behaviour. If there is no inconsistency of any kind, the child should quickly become aware of what particular consequences follow what behaviours on his part.

The need for an individual approach Behaviour modification programmes are designed especially for particular children, and therefore one should observe the child before determining his or her programme.

The child controls his own contingencies Once the child clearly understands what consequences will follow particular behaviour, then he is able to exert his own control within the situation (which is probably something he always does anyway). Once he clearly understands that consequences he wants will follow behaviour the teacher wants, then that behaviour will be forthcoming.

The important principle of reinforcement The term 'reinforcement' means whatever consequence makes behaviour likely to be repeated (positive reinforcement) or whatever consequence makes behaviour unlikely to be repeated (negative reinforcement). By controlling reinforcement situations in the classroom, the teacher can control the child's behaviour. In doing so, the teacher is aiming to hand over appropriate control to the child, once the child appreciates the limits the teacher is setting.

Does the application of reinforcement principles mean that we are bribing the child? No, because bribery implies corruption, and there is no intention whatever to corrupt the child. Nobody does anything without the expectation of some kind of positive reinforcement. The child is already being reinforced in one way or another for his naughty behaviour. Instead of this, we have to find a means of reinforcing good behaviour rather than bad.

The individual aspect of reinforcement It is very important to keep this in mind. Merely to say 'Well done' is not necessarily reinforcing to the child; nor is it necessarily reinforcing to cuddle him or her, give sweets, house points, etc. Children's needs differ and we have to discover for each child what particular measures act as reinforcements.

Reinforcers are useless if they are not contingent If reinforcement techniques are used in haphazard and slapdash ways, they will never be effective. It is important that particular rewards or particular punishments should follow specific behaviours, and that they are not used randomly and haphazardly. Once a particular reinforcement technique has been decided upon, it should be used consistently until the teacher is sure it is not working, when it can be abandoned.

The crucial function of attention as a reinforcer Most children prefer to be attended to rather than to be ignored, even if the attention consists of disapproval. Many children enjoy being singled out, even though it may be for blame. Since attention is a powerful reinforcer, it follows that the logical way to use attention is when the child is being good, and not when he is being naughty. Many children in school are able to get themselves attended to only if they misbehave. It is far better that they should receive attention when they are being good. If behaviour becomes too troublesome to be ignored, then time-out technique should be used.

Principles of classroom behaviour management

Class management principles depend upon the fact that behaviour is determined by its consequences. What follows any particular behaviour is likely to determine whether it is repeated. If this is so, it follows that teachers can bring about a particular type of behaviour by ensuring that they control its consequences. The teacher is in a powerful position for managing his or her classroom effectively.

Positive reinforcement By the systematic presentation of pleasant consequences for children adopting particular behaviour, a teacher can rapidly make acceptable behaviour occur more often. The major problem is to determine for each child which particular consequence is positively reinforcing. If the teacher does not discover this accurately, then the behaviour modification programme is likely to be ineffective.

Positive reinforcement and remedial teaching Many children with serious learning difficulties continue to fail because their

efforts do not receive a high enough degree of positive reinforcement: indeed they are often given negative reinforcement.
There is considerable evidence that, where children are continually positively reinforced, and never negatively reinforced
either by criticism or exasperation or similar behaviour that
they find unwelcome, they will rapidly make progress even if
they have previously failed to do so for several years. Thus the
material given to the child should interest him and should not
be too difficult for him to cope with, and his efforts at coping
should be aided in any way that helps to simplify the task and
make it rewarding. If negative reinforcement is completely
excluded, the child will progress positively.

Negative reinforcement Consequences of this nature will produce avoidance behaviour. For instance, if a child's reading
book is too hard, if his teacher or parents become exasperated
with him, if other children ridicule him, if he does not see
himself making satisfactory progress through his book, if he
has been on the same book for a long time, etc., etc., the child
will try to avoid reading. The reinforcement is negative
because it does not encourage the child to read: it encourages
him not to want to read.

By the same token, various types of negative reinforcement
can be used to discourage behaviour that one does not want
from the child, such as aggressiveness, unruliness or shouting.

Extinction If the contingencies are so arranged that positive
reinforcement does not follow particular behaviour, or if negative reinforcement invariably follows particular behaviour,
then that behaviour will be extinguished and will disappear.
The control of these contingencies is in the hands of the
teacher or whoever is dealing with the child, and the most
aberrant classroom behaviour can be modified by means of an
optimistic approach and the systematic application of appropriate reinforcement principles.

Systematic procedures It is essential that the teacher should be
systematic in using behaviour modification principles. The
systematic procedures imply (1) objective observation; (2)
analysis of the data derived from observation; and (3) the
application of systematic treatment principles derived from
the analysis.

Direct observation If a teacher is worried by a particular child and his behaviour, then it is essential that she should take written notes of the child's behaviour and events that follow the child's behaviour over a given period, say half an hour a day for a week, although it may well be possible to manage on one half hour of observation alone (an example is given later in this chapter). It is essential to observe the situation objectively, and to write down a complete description of precisely what happens, which can then be taken away and analysed.

Analysis of data derived from observation When the teacher does this, she is basically looking for answers to the following questions: What does the child do? What does he do that is unacceptable? What does he do that is acceptable? What reinforcement does he receive for doing unacceptable things? What reinforcement does he receive for doing acceptable things? How can the teacher, by manipulating contingencies of reinforcement, bring about a greater occurrence of acceptable, and the disappearance of unacceptable, behaviour?

Once the situation has been analysed in this way, the teacher should be able to see how to manipulate the consequences of certain behaviours so as to encourage the more frequent occurrence of some and the disappearance of others.

Systematic treatment procedures After analysing the situation in this way the teacher should systematically apply certain predetermined consequences to certain behaviour on the child's part, and she will be able to observe how effective these are. She must be consistent in her measures.

It is likely that the analysis of observational material will also enable certain changes to be made perhaps in the structure of the classroom, seating arrangements, and so forth, in order to increase positive reinforcement for acceptable behaviour and decrease it for unacceptable.

The teacher does not need to go on consistently reinforcing for considerable periods, at least not as part of the systematic schedule. She will need to apply the reinforcement pattern fairly rigidly in the early stages of treatment, but the actual need for reinforcement of a deliberate kind will become considerably more intermittent as time goes by, and can soon be withdrawn altogether. Once the child gets in the habit of doing the right thing, he will do it automatically, purely from force of habit.

Making best use of conditions for learning There are two basic principles in this: (1) Are the materials appropriate to the child? (2) Are the consequences of the child's efforts positively reinforcing? If these two essentials are met, then all children should be able to make positive learning progress.

It follows from this that, if the teacher can find some kind of reinforcement principle that produces benefit for all the children, then the whole group will do far better than if the rewards are handed out to a few only – say the top five. What reinforcement principles can be applied to the class as a whole and to each individual? If satisfactory answers can be found to this crucial question, then a happy class will almost certainly develop.

The principle of successive approximations Children learn best by easy stages, where the hurdles they are expected to jump are not too high for them. This is the basic principle of programmed learning, which is itself derived as a means of helping the instruction programme to fit the individual child. If children are working on materials appropriate to their skill, at an appropriate pace, they should also be moving forward and never standing still or slipping back. They should have a consistent level of regular reinforcement for their efforts.

Effective control of child behaviour: some tips for teachers

Specify accurately what behaviour you want to change or stop. Remember the importance of establishing the base line. What is happening now and what would you like in its place? What target behaviour are you aiming for? What base line behaviour are you observing? What systematic treatment can you inaugurate? Be sure to follow these important principles:

(1) *If other children are affected by the child's behaviour under treatment, get them out of the way.* An alternative is to remove the offending child (see section on time-out behaviour).

(2) *Don't get excited.* Shouting at children may frighten or antagonise them, but it seldom has any long-term effect on their behaviour.

(3) *It is important to keep records.* This particularly applies to observation sessions when base lines are being established.

(4) *It is important to be consistent.* Don't relent too soon. Give treatment a chance to work.

(5) *Take one step at a time*. Otherwise the treatment situation may become too complex.

(6) *Attend to good behaviour and reward it*. This is the concept of positive reinforcement.

(7) *Desirable behaviour should be gradually shaped*. One may do this by manipulating rewards in a constructive way.

(8) *Keep children interested*. Give them plenty of variety.

(9) *Be interested in them*. They will respond far better if you are, and don't just want them to keep quiet and out of the way.

(10) *Be firm and gentle at the same time*. Don't scream and rage. But don't be weak either.

(11) *Don't waste time in a lot of useless talk*. Action is far more effective. One should state the sanction once and then act upon it, or alternatively one may leave the child to work out the sanction for himself without telling him about it.

(12) *Never despair*. If you do you've lost. Never let the child blackmail you emotionally.

(13) *At all times try to remain objective, detached and cool*. The more you can, the more successful you'll be.

(14) *Be prepared for the child's behaviour to get worse before it gets better*. If children are being troublesome, they usually become very annoyed if adults do not react in the distracted way they have come to expect. When the child's behaviour does get worse, hold your ground (see principle 4).

(15) *Show the child that the world still goes on, irrespective of how he behaves*. This is the most effective message you can get across.

'Time-out' treatment for difficult classroom behaviour

It was pointed out earlier that an alternative to removing other children from the problem child one is dealing with, is to remove the offending child himself. This section explains the time-out treatment. The procedure is designed for use where the classroom behaviour of certain children becomes intolerable or nearly so. It is designed to bring about more acceptable behaviour in the child and also *relief for the teacher*.

The teacher should establish clearly in her own mind what behaviour she is or is not prepared to accept from the child. It should be made very clear to the child himself what he will not be allowed to do.

If the child persists in doing what the teacher has forbidden, he should be removed without fuss and placed in another room in school, possibly with the Head or Secretary. He should be told once only why he has been removed from the classroom, and apart from this *should be spoken to as little as possible*. There is ample evidence that children's difficult behaviour is often related to their need for a lot of attention, and it is therefore a very good practice in dealing with difficult behaviour to attend to the child as little as possible. The Head or Secretary or whoever is in charge of the child should proceed with his work and not indulge in conversation with him. If the child should draw attention to himself by difficult behaviour, this should be ignored. No work should be set and the child should be left with nothing to do for a predetermined period of time – perhaps initially ten minutes for an infant, proportionately longer for older ones. The child should be returned to the classroom, again without fuss or talk, at the end of the time-out period.

If difficult behaviour persists on return to the classroom, precisely the same procedure should be carried out. If need be, the period of time out may be extended to fifteen or twenty minutes or even more. There should be no concern about what the child is missing educationally during this time, as the gain to the rest of the class will more than outweigh such considerations, and in any case it is not envisaged that this technique will need to be employed for very long.

Apart from telling the child what he is not to do and pointing out to him in a matter-of-fact way when he has failed to obey instructions, the child should not be given long lectures about his behaviour, and indeed discussion about such matters should be kept to the absolute minimum. There should be no anger or distress shown at any time, and other children should not be allowed to form the impression that the particular child's behaviour is causing any distress to his teachers.

Within the classroom, the troublesome child should be talked to and attended to when he is behaving well, not when he is behaving badly. Bad behaviour should be ignored until it becomes intolerable, whereupon time-out action should be taken. Good behaviour, hard work, diligence, etc., should be attended to and praised.

When the child is aggressive or violent towards other children, he should not be continually rebuked about it. He may be told once that he has done wrong, and if punishment is needed it should consist of time out along the lines mentioned above. It is far more effective if attention is given to the child who has been hurt rather than to the child who has done the hurting. The child who has been hurt should be deliberately and ostentatiously made a fuss of in the presence of the child who has done the hurting. The child who has done the hurting should be ignored if possible, but if this is not possible then time-out procedure should be followed, after the child who has been hurt has been made a fuss of.

Intolerable behaviour in the classroom should be met by exclusion from the classroom. The period of exclusion should be made as dull and boring as possible. No work should be set, and no conversation should take place with the child concerned. He should be supervised, however, at all times.

An illustrative case

R was an Indian boy, six years old. He was referred by his school, which had separate infant and junior departments, because he was proving so disruptive in the classroom that his teacher felt she could not cope with him any longer, despite her considerable teaching experience. The headmaster had interviewed the father in school, and he had reported that the child behaved similarly at home and that this had been a long-term problem. The boy had even been disruptive in nursery school before starting at the infant school. The father was agreeable to the boy's being seen by a psychologist as soon as possible.

Interview with class teacher, Mrs B Mrs B was primarily concerned to have some help with her problem, and to feel that someone was taking an interest and helping her. She needed a means of analysing her difficulties, and some kind of guide about action she might take. She described R as being very aggressive and unable to form relationships with other children. When he did form one, it was primarily because he wanted something from the children concerned. Then he would become very aggressive and force things away from them. Mothers were complaining to Mrs B that their little girls were afraid to come to school because R kept hitting them. R improved to some extent the longer he was in Mrs B's class, but when he had to go into hospital for a short stay he came back more violent and aggressive than ever. He was reported to be quiet for certain periods, and then to burst out when he was thwarted by other children, however mildly. Once having become aggressive, R would continue to be in a bad mood for the rest of the day. He was reported to be very demanding of Mrs B's attention, and to be aware that she would not smack him but tended to cuddle him at times because of his evident need for attention. At first R would resist the cuddles, but later came to enjoy them. He was said not to be aggressive towards Mrs B.

Mrs B felt that R was extremely bright. He had apparently been in a nursery since he was two, from 7.30 a.m. to 6.30 p.m., because both parents were out at work. Other children from the same nursery were said to have shown signs of being difficult. From the outset of R's attendance at infant school the other children showed fear of him, and at home his parents were said to be completely unable to control him. R was said to be extremely aggressive in the street near his home, and to be frustrated by the fact that he had to do an hour's school work for father after he got home at night. He had a two-year-old sibling who was bidding fair to follow in his brother's footsteps.

Father was said to work on nights, and to have to be woken by R on return from school. On one occasion R was said to have thrown a brick through the window to wake father. He was very obsessed with matches and fire, and would occasionally bring matches to school. He reported to Mrs B that he lit a fire in a dog kennel during the school holidays, and he once lit a match in the school playground. He always seemed to have a lot of money to spend, and certainly did not lack material possessions.

In school R was placed in a class of only twenty-four children, and this made him reasonably manageable and helped to bring about some improvement in his behaviour, but the rest of the class was quite lively and occasionally would egg him on to do naughty things. The kinds of naughty things he would do included throwing handfuls of Lego bricks through the classroom window. He was known to lead dinner ladies a merry dance at school mealtimes.

The cuddling that R received from his teacher appeared to be altering his behaviour to some extent in that he was developing a propensity to cuddle the girls in his class, and it was interesting that the girls concerned did not reject him when this happened.

Brief playground observation When R's class was observed walking into school from the playground, it was interesting that R indulged in a lot of falling-about behaviour. He was clearly doing a great deal of attention-seeking, and was aware of the fact that a stranger was watching the group as a whole, though not aware that he himself was being specifically watched. Several children went out of their way to placate him during this time, and there was a lot of interaction between R and other children. He seemed to occupy a dominant position within the social group.

Classroom observation: about twenty-five minutes from 11.35 to 12 o'clock The children were given some drawings to do, and soon, at about 11.40, R came up to the teacher to show what he had been doing. Mrs B sent him back to his place, which was at the nearest desk to her table, right in front of her. R had no one sitting beside him, but two other children, a boy and a girl, were seated opposite in adjacent desks. The timetable of his behaviour (though he was not aware that he was under observation) was as follows:

11.40   Went up to the teacher to show his initial drawing efforts.

11.42   Stood up and leaned over the desk to the two children opposite, whom he engaged in conversation. He had to stretch over considerably in order to do this. Clearly R is a boy who needs a lot of space and to spread himself a good deal. He is a big lad physically, and probably quite strong.

11.43   Up again, talking to the children opposite.

11.43¾ Up again.

11.44   Up again.

11.44½ Up again.

11.45   Up again. Fiddling with crayon box. It was noticeable that the crayon box was right beside R, so that if either of the other two children in his group wanted a crayon he had to come and ask for it.

11.46¼ Up again. Constantly wanting attention from the children opposite. Constantly showing his drawing to them.

11.46¾ Up again. Demanding attention.

11.47 Up again.

11.47½ Up again.

11.47¾ Up again.

(Only two other children had as yet stood up at all, one opposite R and one not near him.)

11.48 Up again.

11.48¼ Up again (one other child got up at the same time in another part of the room).

11.48¾ Up again. Showing his drawing to Mrs B again.

11.49 Up again, pestering the two children opposite him.

11.50 Up again.

11.50½ Up again to challenge a boy who borrowed a crayon from him; this was a boy from a desk some distance from R's. Immediately went across to the boy's desk and grabbed the crayon back.

11.51 Up again, looking round truculently.

11.51¼ Up again, pestering Mrs B with his drawing. (Three other children got up at around the same time, two of them going to see Mrs B.)

11.52½ Up again, speaking with children opposite about crayons.

11.53 Up again. (Another boy got up at the same time. There were twenty-one other children in the class-room.)

11.54 Up again.

11.54½ Up again, taking his drawing to another set of desks to show to other children.

11.55¾ Up again. It was noticeable that R was keeping the crayon box to himself the whole time, and was extremely unwilling to let other children use the crayons.

11.56¼ Up again.

11.57¼ Up again.

11.58½ Again pestering Mrs B, this time about whether or

not he should put his name on his drawing.

12.01   The other children had all left the room by this time to go for dinner. R was the last to leave, and did not attempt to line up with the rest. He put his things away and hurried downstairs after the other children had all left the classroom.

The behaviour-modification approach to this problem Basically the questions we have to ask here are what reinforcement R receives for (i) his attention-seeking behaviour; (ii) his hyperactive behaviour; (iii) his aggressive behaviour; (iv) his demand to control available materials such as crayons; (v) his generally dominant behaviour towards other children; (vi) his attempts to create a special situation for himself which is different from that of other children: for example his obvious feeling that he does not need to line up with the others but can go down for his lunch when he feels like it. The answers to these questions will suggest possible lines of treatment that the teacher might adopt.

How the Educational Psychologist analysed this situation

(1) R's constantly obtrusive behaviour is not acceptable within the classroom because it disrupts continuing activities and distracts the teacher and other children. The reinforcement for this behaviour is the attention given to it by other children and by the teacher. Obviously the teacher is available for children who need attention, but equally obviously in this particular instance R's demands are unreasonable. The following action was suggested:

(a) R should *not* be in the seat nearest to Mrs B, but might well be placed in the seat furthest from her. Instead of having first call on the teacher's attention he should have the least call, at any rate by virtue of the physical arrangement of the classroom. If R likes to sit near Mrs B, then being allowed to sit there should depend upon whether his behaviour is acceptable in other respects, e.g. whether he sits quietly in his place and gets on with his work instead of disturbing other children.

(b) Other children should not be so readily available for R to pester. In other words, the two children sitting opposite R should be placed further away from him, so that he cannot disrupt their work and make demands on them quite so readily. It should be made clear to R quietly and without fuss that the other children are being removed from his immediate vicinity until he has learned to sit in his place and get on with his work in the way that the other children do. When R has learned this, the other children can be returned to his vicinity.

(c) The teacher should not reinforce R's approaches to her unless his other classroom behaviour is acceptable. She should give her attention to R when he is sitting in his place and getting on with his work, and not when he is continually coming up to her desk to make demands over and above those of other children.

(d) R might possibly be given rewards for sitting quietly at his desk, such as house points or extra teacher attention.

(2) R's dominant behaviour should be tackled in a determined way. In no circumstances should he be allowed to take charge of the crayon box until he has demonstrated that he can control the crayons in a fair and democratic way, so that other children are not penalised by his domineering behaviour. The crayon box should be taken out of R's charge immediately, and he should be given only short spells in charge of it until he learns to do so properly. Any aggression towards other children resulting from their wish to borrow crayons should be punished by withdrawing from R the right of being in charge of the crayon box for a sufficient period to be a positive deterrent to such aggressive behaviour.

(3) Behaviour such as not lining up with the other children and not going down to dinner at the proper time should be penalised by making this boy wait for his dinner after other children have been served for an equivalent length of time to his lateness. Alternatively one might double the time or even treble it – the major consideration being which treatment is most effective.

(4) Mrs B might continue to show affection and attention to this boy, if she wishes and thinks it helpful, but in no circumstances when he is behaving or has behaved badly. Any positive reinforcements, such as kind words or cuddling, should be given only when R's behaviour has been good and

in no circumstances when it has been bad.

(5) In a general sense the whole class can work to a system of house points or some other token reward system for good behaviour, and efforts can be made to involve R closely in such a system so that he becomes motivated to behave well instead of badly.

(6) Similar tactics can be employed at home with R, assuming that his parents are cooperative and that they can be trained in the use of such techniques.

The analysis of R's situation given above and the suggestions for treatment made were drawn up before his treatment programme began, and were printed and circulated for the information of other teachers before it was known whether or not the suggestions were effective. At a teachers' meeting some weeks later it transpired that Mrs B was present, unknown to the psychologist circulating the case study, and it was very gratifying to hear that the suggestions made had been carried out by her and had proved particularly effective.

The points illustrated in this case study are (1) the need to describe situations adequately by observation before any treatment pattern is sought; (2) the need to look for existing reinforcement patterns which control children's behaviour; and (3) the value of rational and carefully-thought-out approaches to child management problems, whether at home or at school, and how these procedures can be very much improved by careful situation analysis and by consistent treatment. Additionally, if particular treatments fail, the same routine of observation and analysis can be carried out again and alternative methods used (though in this case such further observations were not needed). The important considerations are that situations should be closely analysed and experimental treatments tried on a consistent basis.

Follow-up to the case

R was observed again in the classroom, again over a twenty-five minute period, ten months after the initial twenty-five-minute observation. He was by this time placed with a different teacher. The notes of the observation session ran as follows:

11.35   Wandering about the classroom in a rather swaggering fashion calling out that he wanted a rubber. Went to Mrs D to try to obtain one, after an initial tour of the classroom on the same mission.

11.39   Up again. Showing his work to Mrs D.

11.41   Up again. Wandering around, looking for 'the rubber' again. Wandering to every table in the room.

11.43½   Up again. Talking to children on his table. Looking around the room. Animated conversation with a boy sitting next to him (it should be noted that quite a lot of children are wandering about the room, this being a very free classroom atmosphere).

11.45   Flicked something at a girl to attract her attention. Asked her if she had the rubber. Knocked his chair over in a typically ostentatious gesture.

11.46   Up again. Lining up in the queue at the teacher's desk. Remains a boy who seems to need a good deal of physical activity.

11.48   Reaching over for a rubber which a child near him had. Makes a great play of needing the rubber and using it frequently.

11.49   In queue at the teacher's desk again.

11.50   Up again to see the teacher.

11.51   Rebuked by Mrs D who told him that he had only a little time left to finish his work. Stood up almost immediately to look round again.

11.52   Sat rocking his chair from side to side.

11.55   Went out with the rest of the children to get ready for dinner.

Following the second observation session, the present status of the case was summarised as follows:

We still have a picture of an attention-seeking boy who remains physically very active and who constantly has to be acting upon his environment in one way or another. However, there is certainly a considerable improvement by comparison with the previous observation period. When seen ten months before, there were twenty-eight instances of R getting up and pestering either his teacher or other children; on this occasion there were only ten instances over roughly the same period of time. Even the ratio of twenty-eight to ten did not give a true picture of R's improvement, since during the former observation period not many children were moving about at all, whilst in the latter observation most of the children were very active. Thus even in a situation where children were being very active as a matter of course, R was still only on his feet on ten occasions whereas previously there had been as many as twenty-eight with most of the children sitting quietly at their desks. Thus there is quite definitely a marked improvement in R so far as moving about is concerned and although the second observation period had only seen a very limited sample of his behaviour, R's new teacher in fact confirmed that the improvement noted had actually taken place.

R still presented as a boy who required firm treatment. He had always seemed to be thoroughly spoiled and he consistently behaved under observation as someone used to manipulating people and situations. He would certainly need to have it made plain to him that he would not get away with difficult or obnoxious behaviour and it was pleasing to see that the new teacher was utilising a firm and consistent approach to him. R was particularly difficult at the time of the second interview with visiting dinner ladies and it was suggested that he should be made to wait for a long time for his dinner if he continued to be disruptive in those circumstances. It was felt that he was intelligent enough to speedily appreciate what things he would not be allowed to get away with, so that his behaviour would modify accordingly.

R's home was visited round about the same time as the second observation was made. It seemed that R's parents were not sufficiently firm in dealing with him and the need for firmness and consistency was also stressed to them. R remained very aggressive with other children at school and with his younger sister at home and it was considered essential that these aggressive approaches towards others should be speedily stopped. One method of dealing with aggressive behaviour in schools is outlined in the section on time-out treatment.

Remedial teaching as behaviour modification

We have already discussed the relevance of the behaviour modification approach to remedial teaching. The step-by-step approach that characterises programmed learning applies particularly to remedial teaching. If this is broken down into small steps, then there is frequent reinforcement for the learner. If the steps are consistently within the learner's capability, then there is frequent positive reinforcement, and with this there is inevitably successful learning. Thus it is essential that material should be tailored to the needs of the learner, and situations deliberately created in which he or she can succeed.

If one analyses reading in relation to remedial teaching, it is, with care, possible to devise an effective programme. Apart from the need to find suitable reading books within the learner's capability, it is also possible to programme particular pages in an effective way before those pages are tackled, and to erect scaffolding for success by talking about the content in advance, by teaching certain words in advance, or by helping the child along in a fairly subtle and smooth manner if he is reading aloud. Thus the teacher creates a situation where the learner does most of the work, and the book itself is a complex learning experience rather than a ritual incantation. The materials may be good, but they are better if used effectively.

The learner likes to observe his progress Assuming the basic premise, that the teacher tries to ensure a minimum of failure for the learner, one can still show the child's progress in a graphic way. If page one is read the first time with twenty words right and five errors, one can represent these by means of ticks and crosses in boxes, and one can illustrate a better performance at the second attempt and a better one still at the third. In the same way the child's progress through the book can be mapped in terms of words read accurately and words read inaccurately, care always being taken to ensure that the former outweighs the latter. One might save only the child's best performance on each page, or keep every performance on each page so that he can look back on his progress. One can also keep account of books read, new words learnt, etc.

The remedial teacher will obviously wish to develop his own written work to some extent, but certain published English work books, for example those by Ridout, can be of great help. They are valuable because the pupil can work on them unsupervised, particularly if the stage is set by the teacher beforehand, through the preliminary working-through of material and so forth, and indeed the pupil can work on material of this kind at home as well. Even grossly retarded children of twelve, thirteen, or fourteen are willing to spend a lot of their own time on this kind of work-book material if the work is within their grasp, if their remedial teacher works through it with them before and after, or at least after, and if it is regularly marked and assessed.

For Mathematics programming, books such as the *Yardsticks* published by Nelson enable the teacher to discover fairly rapidly at what stage of arithmetical development the child is stagnating, so that particular areas of weakness can be concentrated upon and worked through in a systematic and programmed fashion. Such books are eminently useful for diagnosis as well as for practice, and they also make the way ahead clear both for the teacher and for the learner, even if the learner is well behind his age or class group at some particular time. Aids of this kind are particularly useful because of the structure into which they are incorporated which takes a great deal of the hit-or-miss element out of remedial teaching.

Programmed texts These can be obtained both in reading and arithmetic and indeed in most subjects of the curriculum. They can be obtained at fairly elementary and also at fairly advanced levels. Some programmes are linear and simple, others branching and complex, but they have in common a basic principle, namely that learning progresses in small steps and that the learner is positively reinforced as frequently as possible. Additionally the learning is cemented as frequently as possible because, particularly in branching programmes, the learner will not proceed to the next step until he has mastered the present one.

Teaching machines These often comprise organised programmes that might have been in book form, but are incorporated in machines by way of variation. Reinforcement is sometimes by visual checking following the turning of a knob, but certain devices for electronic checking of answers also exist, where for instance a green light might flash for a correct answer, and a red light for an incorrect one. Needless to say, this kind of learning gadget is often very attractive to youngsters who have had failures with conventional pens or pencils.

Other teaching machines, such as the Language Master, operate on a different principle by presenting learning material in a regulated and modulated form for easy learning, without requiring the learner to select correct answers or to follow organised linear or branching programmes. Machines of this type are very valuable not only because they encourage systematic learning, but also because they incorporate auditory as well as visual aspects of reading skills. Again in this situation the learner progresses by physical manipulation, which seems to be a very strong aid to learning for some retarded pupils.

Many other types of learning aids exist, some programmed, some not, but the principle of programming is an important one, and it is probably true to say that if the material is not programmed, then the teacher will have to programme it if he wishes the learner to make maximum progress. Even if it is programmed, the teacher may have to adapt it for the particular child so that the scaffolding set up is the most appropriate and effective for him.

Afterword

The techniques of behaviour modification outlined above are applicable in many instances where behaviour problems arise in school. In other instances, particularly at secondary school level, a counselling approach, with pupil or family or both, may be more appropriate.

FURTHER READING

G. J. Blackman and A. Silberman, *Modification of Child Behaviour* Wasworth Publishing Co., 1971.

R. N. Browning and D. O. Stover, *Behaviour Modification in Child Treatment*, Aldine–Atherton, 1971.

A. M. Graziano (Ed.), *Behaviour Therapy with Children*, Aldine Publishing Co., 1971.

A. M. Graziano, *Behaviour Therapy with Children, 2*, Aldine Publishing Co., 1975.

M. L. Meacham and A. E. Wiesen, *Changing Classroom Behaviour*, International Text Book Co., 1969.

James A. Poteet, *Behaviour Modification: A Practical Guide for Teachers*, Unibooks, University of London Press Ltd, 1973.

J. Presland, 'Helping the Maladjusted Child', *Journal of the Association of Educational Psychologists*, Vol. 3, No. 2, Autumn 1972.

J. Presland, 'Dealing with Disruptive Behaviour in the Classroom', *Journal of the Association of Educational Psychologists*, Vol. 3, No. 3, 1973.

Epilogue

GERALD HAIGH

Finishing this book with a paper on behaviour modification serves, I feel, to emphasise the great and ultimately helpful variety of points of view which have been brought to bear on our subject. My own aim throughout has been to let the reader see how wide is the spectrum of approaches, secure always in the knowledge that each and every contributor is a successful and caring educationalist.

To some extent, the variety of approach reflects the differences between human beings. Joe Newman's way works because he is Joe Newman. He could not easily work like Richard Martin any more than Richard could work as Joe does – and what is more important, if under some decree either were forced to work like the other, the end result would be unhappy and probably not very successful. Those who make sweeping pronouncements about what is best for our children, and about the 'failure' of this method or the 'success' of that, would do well to remember this. It is, after all, a very elementary fact of human life.

It follows, quite obviously, that neither I nor any of the contributors expect any reader, however anxious for help he may be, to swallow any of our ideas wholesale, or to become, overnight, a carbon copy of those whose methods seem to work. Any teacher, like any human being, is the sum of his experiences. What we have tried to do here is to add to this experience in a direct and pointed way.

Further Reading

Few writers in education have really wanted to identify separately the issue of discipline – for all the reasons which have been repeated through this book. Thus, it is not easy to suggest further reading beyond the references which some of the contributing authors give.

One book which does actually mention discipline on the cover is *Beyond Control? A study of discipline in the comprehensive school* by Paul Francis (Allen & Unwin 1975). This is a very personal account of problems and possible solutions. Before that there was *Discipline in Schools* edited by Turner (Ward Lock 1973). *Secondary Modern Discipline* by R. Farley (Black 1960) is as stern as its title suggests, but worth a look.

As you might expect, most of the books intended for new teachers say something about discipline, even if they shy from the actual word. My own *Beginning Teaching* (Pitman 1972) is one example, and *Learner Teacher* by N. Otty (Penguin 1972) is another.

The Reluctant Adolescent, again mine (Temple Smith 1976) has chapters about order and authority. The progressive case is well represented in books such as *A Last Resort* by Peter Newell (Penguin 1972) which is a criticism of corporal punishment, and *Education Without Schools* edited by Peter Buckman (Souvenir Press 1973), which is a collection of papers which together largely reject the whole authoritarian basis of formal schooling.

A number of interested bodies – unions and education authorities – have also put out documents on discipline, of which *Disruptive and Violent Behaviour in Schools* published by the Devon County Council in 1975 is a good example.

Some of the most illuminating and perhaps in the end most

helpful writing on this subject is to be found in fiction. *The Rainbow* by D. H. Lawrence (Penguin edition 1970) has some searing descriptions of a hostile and barely controlled authoritarian confrontation in school. *Kestrel for a Knave* by Barry Hines (Penguin edition 1969) ought also to be required reading for those teachers who have not yet awoken to the pressures which make adolescent boys and girls tick and go off bang. *Roaring Boys* by Edward Blishen (Panther Books edition 1972) is also an excellent piece of catharsis for the teacher who is thinking that it only happens to him.

Notes on Contributors

Gerald Haigh is head of Henry Bellairs CE Middle School, in North Warwickshire. Since 1961 he has taught in primary, secondary modern, comprehensive and middle schools. He is the author of numerous books and articles on educational matters including *Teaching Slow Learners*, Temple Smith 1977.

Carlton Duncan is Deputy Head and Director of Personal Development at Sidney Stringer School and Community College in Coventry. A Jamaican by birth, he has been in this country since 1961. Since that time he has, after university and teacher training, held a variety of increasingly senior posts in secondary schools.

Ron Fawcett is Principal Educational Psychologist for Warwickshire and has worked in the County for fourteen years. He is a Lancashire man by birth and attended Manchester Grammar School and Manchester University and took his training in Educational Psychology at the University of London. He is an Associate Member of the British Psychological Society and a former Honorary Treasurer and Executive Committee Member of the Association of Educational Psychologists. His major aim in psychology is to try to reconcile the different approaches implicit in behaviour modification on the one hand and counselling on the other.

Bob Jelley has been teaching for five years. He is a fourth year class teacher in a Warwickshire Middle School for pupils aged eight to twelve.

Richard Martin and **Jenifer Smith** are team teachers at Countesthorpe College, Leicestershire. Richard Martin has been teaching for eleven years, the last eight at Countesthorpe. He is married with three children. Jenifer Smith has been teaching for eight years, the last six in the Countesthorpe teams.

Richard W. Mills is a Senior Lecturer in the Education Department at Westhill College, Birmingham, and author of *Teaching English across the Ability Range*, Ward Lock Educational, 1977.

Joseph Newman is Head of Matthew Arnold School, Oxford. He came to this post six years ago having previously taught in two grammar schools and a comprehensive school. Before that he served as an officer in the Royal Air Force.

Henry Pluckrose is headteacher of Prior Weston Primary School, in London EC1. He has taught for twenty-five years in inner-city schools. He is the author of over thirty books for children and twenty books for teachers and parents, and was until recently editor of the monthly *Art and Craft in Education*.

Peter Woods is Senior Lecturer in the Sociology of Education at the Open University. He has taught in primary and secondary schools in Norfolk, London and Yorkshire. Dr Woods has written and edited numerous books and articles on education, the most recent being *The Divided School*, Routledge and Kegan Paul, 1979.